MW00411807

Iva
Sept. 6, 2015
Ladies Class
Teacher Amanda Stephans
1st class Oct 11

So You Want to be Happy?

Eric L. Owens

Second Edition

ISBN: 1481966448
ISBN-13:978-1481966443

DEDICATION

This book is dedicated to my wife and daughters. Thanks, Vanessa, for all of your love and support. You have been and are an amazing person. Your love and concern for people make you beautiful inside and out. I have learned a lot from you and hope to learn more. Thank you for your commitment to our family. I know of no one who cares for and protects her family more. You are more than a wife you are a genuine friend. Your ear is always appreciated. Your confidence in me is unwavering. I thank God that I was privileged to marry you. You make my life sweet. Part of the blessing of our being together is having our wonderful girls.

Girls, this is for you. Brittany, Breania, and Bethany, I love you girls so much. I know you know, but I just wanted to say it. You girls truly are a heritage from the Lord. I cannot imagine life without you. You all have made us so proud. Thanks for listening to all of those life lessons. Thanks for being willing to follow. Thanks for your care and encouragement. Thanks for making me a better man. Being your father is a labor of love. I love you.

CONTENTS

ACKNOWLEDGMENTS

I must acknowledge my family. Our father and mother taught us to love one another thank you both Dad I love you. Every member of my family is special, and I love you all; thank you for helping me become the man I am. Mama, you are great; thank you for everything. You are, in my estimation, the greatest mother anyone could ever be blessed to have. I have a big brother like no other, Greg; thanks for looking out for me. Thanks for loving me, Arletha; you are my special dear little sister. I love you and thank you for loving me.

I had the privilege of working with my best friend for over a decade. As iron sharpens iron, Jonathan, you helped me over the years. Your insight and thoughts were invaluable. J., I only hope I helped you as much as you helped me. Love you man.

To the Tuesday Morning Class a great thanks and appreciation is given. You have challenged me and questioned me over the years. You have caused me to think more and study harder as a result. I am indebted to you for broadening my perspective. The foundation you helped me lay is invaluable; thank you. Whatever I write can probably trace its origin to our class.

To the Avondale Elders, past and present, with whom I serve, and labor; thank you. These good men, virtually sight unseen, gave me an opportunity. You have been patient and encouraging--not simply through this material, but our entire work. Thank you for all that you have done and continue to do. Thank you for being my shepherds.

To the Avondale congregation, "thank you" does not seem sufficient. I trust you know my deep affection for you. I am thankful to labor among you. It has been a joy and privilege that I will cherish always. Thank you for your patience as we worked through this material. Thank you for not watching the clock. Thank you for your encouragement. Thank you for your attention, input, questions, and disagreements. It is a joy to share my life with you.

Introduction

Nothing Physical Can Bring Lasting Happiness, Because Nothing Physical Lasts

This is not something you feel. Neither is it something you have to "experience." It is not "better felt than told." We who love the Lord can reclaim what God offers; when we do, those without God will want to have Him as well.

The material will be divided into three sections:

Section 1:
The Failing of Physical Religion (Chapters 1-4)

In these chapters I will share with you why religious people are not happy. Today's religion is failing those who profess it. Its messages and teaching do not differ from the world's messages. The result is that those who profess Christ think, act, and live just like those who make no profession. Lamentably, the world has converted the church and not the other way around.

Section 2:
Focusing on a Spiritual Mindset (Chapters 5-8)

These chapters will concern themselves with a return to a spiritual mindset. Those with God should live differently than those without God. Life is the same for us all, but when the storms of life come, the houses of those who believe should stand.

Remember the wise man built his house upon the Rock. The foolish man did not. The wise man's house stood. The foolish man's house fell. They were not the same.

Section 3:
Finding Genuine Happiness (Chapters 9-13)

In this section we reunite with God. Having identified the problems and changed our minds, we are now ready to reunite with God. God is the only eternal constant in our lives. What He has done in Jesus is sufficient to sustain us in this life, and His promise of heaven is sufficient to sustain us eternally.

Chapter 1

Preaching Prosperity from Pulpits

There Is No Distinction Between Believers and Non-Believers

There are three things you need to know right away about lasting happiness. First, happiness is found in God. You might say, "I know that"; however, even if you have heard that only God can make you happy, you will still not find happiness because you are given so much misinformation about God. The wrong information about God will not make one happy, it will make one miserable. Likely, you have never heard what God actually says about lasting happiness because preachers continue to mislead you about God. I will say more about that later. Thus happiness remains lost to you, even if you are looking for it in God.

Second, lasting happiness is not found on earth. If you are looking here, you will never find it. In the Old Testament book of Ecclesiastes king Solomon searched for lasting happiness. He used the expression "under the sun" to describe the sphere of his search. His search was conducted on earth and he never found happiness. The reason is simple: Lasting happiness is not under the sun, it is beyond the sun. Please do not spend your life searching for lasting happiness in a place where you can never find it.

Third, nothing physical can bring lasting happiness. Nothing physical can bring lasting happiness because nothing physical lasts. What did you get for Christmas three years ago? Do you still enjoy it the way you did when you first got it, or has it already been replaced. I have no doubt you have been looking for happiness. You have just been looking in the wrong place.

Life is life. The basic ingredients are the same for everybody: We are born, we live, and we die. This understanding of life establishes our reality. There have been precious few exceptions to this rule (Enoch [Genesis 5:24; Hebrews 11:5] and Elijah [2 Kings 2:11] come to mind). No one else ever deviates from this dynamic. To be human is to share this reality with every other human.

The conditions of our births differ, the conditions of our lives differ, the reasons for our deaths differ; but everyone will experience the same thing. For some this cycle is measured in seconds or minutes, for most it will be measured in years, but for a few it will be measured in a century.

If our lives be measured in years, and we experience a few of them; we all come to want the same thing: Happiness. We all want to be happy. From babies to seniors, we do not live long, before we want our share of happiness. Unfortunately, most people never feel like they get their share of the stuff. Therefore, one or two things are true of us all: one, we want to be happy; two, we are not.

For all of our inescapable, inevitable sameness of birth, life, and death; there is one very important difference. It is this difference that determines one's happiness--at least it should. Consider this with me: The cycle of life varies in length, quality, comfort, wealth, education, experience, and a host of other things; but none of those have anything to do with whether or not one is happy. We will discuss why in the book; although I will tell you now it is not hard to distinguish between rich unhappy people and poor unhappy people.

What is it? What is the one thing that determines happiness? God! Life is life. We are born, we live we die, the same for us all; but if what the Bible teaches about God be true (and I believe it is), then having God in one's life as opposed to not having God in one's life should be profoundly different.

There is no way to reconcile the thought differently. Life is life for everyone. We are born, we live, we die; but some people have God and others do not. If people without God are happy and people with God are happy then what is the point of God? If people without God are happy and people with God are miserable then God is detrimental. If people with God are happy and people without God are not, then God is the difference and the reason for having God increases exponentially.

Let me be clear; I am not talking about temporary joy. I'm not even talking about a few moments or even years of enjoyment. I'm talking about something deeper. Something much stronger; something the Scripture says God gives. Modern preaching prevents one from finding lasting happiness because it focuses on physical life here and now. It is consumed with life under the sun. Humanity must come to understand that physical things are not signs of spiritual blessings, for even non-believers can buy homes, cars, and toys.

Therefore, a purely physical religion is no different than non-religion. The reason "Christianity" is not growing as it once did is this: There is no distinction between those who profess Christianity and those who deny it. Today's religion provides nothing to which the world can convert--and provides no true motivation; for believers to live faithful lives. Additionally, it provides no light for the church to shine among the world.

If there is one thing that religious people and non-religious people should agree on, it is that their beliefs are not the same. The Bible constantly emphasizes a distinction between God's children and those who are not God's children. The Israelites were God's people; the Gentile world around them was heathens or unbelievers. The distinctions between God's people have always been stark and clear.

In Scripture there is light and darkness. There is good and evil. There is God and the devil. There is the kingdom and the world. The teaching of the Bible is spiritual. God is Spirit (John 4:24). God's word is spiritual (John 6:63). There are the old man of sin and the new man renewed after God (Ephesians 4:20-23). The messages from God are designed to save our souls. His living and active Word changes our character. He renews our minds (Romans 12:1-2). But, the thoughts of men lead to ruin, darkness and destruction (Jeremiah 10:23).

Because of its focus on physical prosperity, typical religious preaching goes out of its way to make no distinction in one's life from the world. With its extreme emphasis on physical prosperity, this preaching sounds the same as the message of people who live without God. It has the same source of success. It has the same morals. It has the same ethics. It teaches the same things. If we are honest, we would have to conclude that it is very difficult--if not impossible--to tell the difference between prosperity preaching, Humanism, or even Atheism.

When asked if atheist were going to hell one very popular preacher said he could not say, he did not judge, he just preached Jesus. Sadly this is an acceptable answer for many who call themselves Christians. This preacher does not preach Jesus if he did he would say what Jesus said about those who do not believe in Him:

- I told you that you would die in your sins, for unless you believe that I am he you will die in your sins. (John 8:24)
- The one who rejects me and does not receive my words has a judge; the word that I have spoken will judge him on the last day. (John 12:48)
- Whoever is not with me is against me, and whoever does not gather with me scatters. (Matthew 12:30)

The prosperity preachers use God's name for their claims; but if you must listen to the messages they preach. Listen closely to the teaching and you will see that there is no distinction between believers and non-believers. In the next chapter we will notice their messages to the masses.

What Do You Think?

1. What kind of preaching is being preached today?
2. Is the Bible respected today, both in the church and out?
3. Why do you think Jesus came to earth?
4. Do believers and non-believers see life the same?
5. How are Christians different from non-Christians?

Chapter 2

Messages for the Masses

"More Will Make You Happy!"

When God's word is taught, believed and lived it will make us happy. However, if we believe things that are not true and strive to live them out in our lives we will be miserable. Scripture says, God's word is truth (John 8:31-32), as we will see prosperity preachers are not preaching the truth. Instead, they have replaced God's truths with messages for the masses that don't even resemble God's word. When one compares what they are preaching to God's word it becomes clear that following these messages cannot make us happy, but might instead cost us our souls. Don't take my word for it, just listen to what is taught.

More Money Will Make You Happy

The first message is simple: If you get lots of money you will be happy! If you were asked, "What is the number one topic preached by prosperity preachers?"; what would your answer be? Would not we all have to say money? There can be no doubt that most religious people see money as an extremely important thing as it relates to their happiness.

They might say that money is not important or that one should not live for money, but when one attends worship service every week and the most preached about topic is money, the result is his developing a deep belief in the god of money.

Ask the average person, religious or non-religious, what he needs most. What do you think the answer will be? The overwhelming answer would be more money. Each believes that as soon as he gets more money he will have joy, happiness, and contentment. He will be complete at last, he will be happy.

I have heard of a church that allows members to buy a lottery ticket upon entering the building for worship. By the end of the service a drawing is held to determine the winner. Do you think money plays an important part of prosperity preaching? Some churches have ATM machines inside. What impact does this have on religious people? Since they are taught that money is so important to life and happiness, of course they spend their lives trying to get more money.

Instead of spiritual pursuits, money is the pursuit. Religious people work themselves to death trying to get more money. Some put themselves into compromising positions. They sacrifice Truth, their ethics, and morality to get more money. Some have lost their freedom trying to get more money. Think about that for a moment. What price tag would you put on your freedom?

Some have their lost their families, striving to get more money. Children are not lost by the state or the church they are lost at home. There are only 24 hours in the day. If we spend our lives trying to make a lot of money, we cannot spend our lives rearing our children. Children need their parents not their presents.

Some continue to live with the consequences of striving to make more money. Some lives may never be the same. We have paid a lot more than we ever gained. Even those who did make lots of money found out an awful truth: Money cannot make you happy, even if you have lots of it. Making money did not work, because that is the wrong place to search for lasting happiness.

Men are searching for meaning, fulfillment, and happiness; and are told that if they had more money, they would find these things. It was and is preached to them every week. That the world has this kind of focus is understandable; regrettably, this is the message from preachers as well.

It would have helped if the Bible were preached to men, then they would have learned about King Solomon. Do you know him? He was the son of David. He went on a search to find lasting happiness in life. He searched for it in money. His search is recorded in the Old Testament book of Ecclesiastes. You should read it.

If happiness were in money, Solomon would have been the happiest man on earth, because he was the richest man on earth. He had silver, gold, and all kinds of treasures. He had men singers and women singers. He was greater than all who were before him and after him. He was a rich, religious man. He could have had anything his heart desired.

What he wanted was happiness. But what he found was that having lots of money did not bring it. In Ecclesiastes 2:1-8, he spoke about his wealth and all he had. After which he made this insightful observation: "Then I considered all that my hands had done and the toil I had expended in doing it, and behold, all was vanity and a striving after wind, and there was nothing to be gained under the sun" (Ecclesiastes 2:9-11).

Prosperity preachers do not tell people that Solomon had it all physically, but he did not have happiness. Instead they keep telling men to tithe, and God will give them a blessing--and when they get that blessing they will be happy at last. Money is not where happiness lives, but people are so consumed with it that they are willing to do just about anything to get it. Friend, this is not from God; it is greed!

It is not wrong for religious people to have money. Money is neither good nor evil. It is a tool. However, "*the love of money* [emph. ELO] is the root of all evil" (1 Timothy 6:10). What is being taught in religion is the love of money. To love money is to be greedy. Greed causes people to lie for money. Greed causes people to steal for money. Chasing after money causes a lot of grief, pain, and sadness--not happiness.

If preachers preached what God said about money, they would tell men that "godliness with contentment is great gain" (1 Timothy 6:6). They would preach, "We brought nothing into this world and it is certain that we can carry nothing out" (1 Timothy 6:7). They would preach this most important point: If we have food and clothing God tells us to be content.

Think long and hard about what God says and what most preachers preach. They might also tell men that the Bible says that those who pursue riches fall into temptation, snares, and traps that plunge people into ruin and destruction. The reason for this is that the love of money is the root of all kinds of evils (1 Timothy 6:6-10); however, they do not preach the Bible, they preach prosperity.

They preach man's best life now. There is no need to hide anymore behind any idea of Jesus and Scripture. Preachers openly tell their hearers that Christianity is about money. One suggested your family is not interested in the Gospel, but show them some money and they will listen. If you show them the money, they will come.

Now, note how far afield that is from Jesus' Message: "Go into all the world and proclaim the Gospel to the whole creation. Whoever believes and is baptized will be saved, but whoever does not believe will be condemned" (Mark 16:15-16).

Jesus never told anybody that He would show them the money. Rather, He came and laid down His life for His sheep (John 10:15). He was "despised and rejected of men" (Isaiah 53:3). "He came unto his own, and his own received him not" (John 1:11). I wonder if He knew all He had to do to win people was to show them the money. You mean he could have avoided Calvary by showing the Pharisees the money.

He had this novel idea of service. He just "went about doing good" (Acts 10:38). He put others before himself. He came to minister not to be ministered unto (Matthew 20:28). He washed the apostle's feet and told them to imitate His humility (John 13:1-17). He also told his apostles that they would always have the poor among them (John 12:8). Have you ever noticed that Jesus did not do in his personal ministry what preachers profess that He does from heaven? When He was on earth, He did not rain money from heaven. He told his followers to go and preach the Gospel (Mark 16:15-16)--not show the world the money. Since Jesus did not teach, show them the money, this message has a different source than God.

Maybe it comes from the depths of hell itself; maybe it comes from the fertile imaginations of false teachers and preachers who are greedy, arrogant, covetous men and women who pimp and prostitute their prevision of the glorious Gospel of Jesus Christ (2 Peter 2:1-4) to simple souls who follow them hoping to one day share in the spoils! I know this: This teaching certainly does not come from Jesus.

These prosperity preachers have been called out about their preaching. They have been questioned about how little it resembles

Jesus' preaching. Amazingly, they have not recanted. They have not apologized. They have not repented. Instead, they have defended their preaching, and the defense of their preaching has been more outrageous even than the preaching. In defense of their doctrine of dollars they have suggested that the Lord had money because He had a treasurer. The implication is that the Lord profited from religion; therefore, they are simply emulating the Lord.

Such a basic lack of Bible knowledge concerning our Lord screams aloud that they should not be handling the Word of God in any capacity, much less trying to teach it to tens of thousands of people.

Preachers are to rightly divide God's Word--handle It right (2 Timothy 2:15). They are not to twist or pervert the Scriptures (2 Peter 3:16). But given this defense it makes me ask, "Have they never read '. . . Foxes have holes, and the birds of the air have nests; but *the Son of man has nowhere to lay his head*?'" (Matthew 8:20). Or maybe they should read that, "... Susanna, and many others, *ministered unto him of their substance* [emph. ELO]" (Luke 8:1-3).

And do they not know that Judas held the bag and was stealing from it (John 12:6). The Lord said that He did not have a place to lay His head. The foxes and birds were better off than He was in this regard. He received help from others because He did not have enough. He was even buried in a borrowed tomb. Wow! For a man with a treasurer, the Lord sure sounds like He was lacking. Did the Lord know His own state?

Prosperity preachers would not be caught dead living like the Lord. They have their private jets, expensive animals, huge homes, and ultra-expensive cars. One boasted of an $18,000 dog, which could respond to commands in three languages, yes sir sounds just like Jesus.

The Lord rode on a borrowed mule. It is sad, but sadder still is the fact that people show up in droves to hear them and fund their lifestyles. Some folks may not admit it, but they show up in part because the prosperity preacher keeps promising that they will soon get their share. The problem is they keep bringing their money and giving it away--and they keep leaving empty handed.

They have not yet figured out that the sermon is one long infomercial. In an infomercial the people making the promises about how to make lots of money are selling the viewer their product, so they (the pitchmen) can make lots of money. It is the same in prosperity preaching: A man keeps showing up and giving the preacher money, and the preacher uses that man's money, as proof that his formula for making money works.

But unlike the infomercials, there is no fine print; the hearer does not get a disclaimer. If he did, it would say, "Results not typical." Or as I like to say, "Everything I'm saying does not really work." The difference is that in infomercials the government makes them put the disclaimer on the TV screen. One cannot help notice that it is always mice type. One would almost think the advertisers do not want the viewer to read it.

The problem for the sermon hearer is that in religion the preacher does not have to provide man a disclaimer, so man keeps showing up hoping that this will be the week that what he says finally comes true. It has not, and it will not. One cannot find happiness in money, even if he is told that God is the One giving him the money.

More Things Will Make You Happy

The second message is connected to the first: Get lots of possessions. Because of the focus on the physical, the lives of religious people mirror the lives of non-religious people. Paul exhorted God's people to be content with food and raiment (1 Timothy 6:6-10), but how many are?

Since money is taught as being supreme, the natural thing to do with money is to buy things. It is hard to believe this message is supposed to come from God. But, just try to find the difference between a person of "faith" and a faithless person these days and you cannot. In short, both believe the one with the most toys wins.

How many preachers have you heard brag about how much stuff they have? What message do the members take from such preaching? It is simple really if I get more stuff I will be happy. I will be like the preacher. God is blessing him, and look at all of his stuff. If I have lots of money, then I can buy lots of stuff. Possessions have become an indication of piety--of course God disagrees with that (1 Timothy 6:3-5); but since men do not hear God's Word; they believe the messages from the preachers is actually coming from God. Sadly, it is not.

That it has influenced us all is easy to see, look around your house. How much stuff do you have? We have so much stuff we often need storage units. But we do not simply have stuff, we have multiplied stuff. We have so much stuff it is hard to keep the house clean anymore. The floor has become the new hamper. We put clothes on the floor and in the closet, we have unworn clothes with tags still on them. Many clothes are bought and discarded without ever being worn.

The closets are full. The attic is full. The basement is full. The garage is full. The storage shed is full. We have double and triple of many of the same things. We acquire the first one, then the new and improved one, and then we get the highly efficient, newest and best one.

Now we need more space, so we can buy more stuff. The reason clothes can be thrown on the floor is because the joy was in buying them not having them. Now that they are home what do they really mean to us? We know things do not make us happy. But we continue to buy them hoping the next thing will.

Another "good," worldly reason to buy more stuff is so our friends will envy us. We want to show all the other religious people how much the Lord is blessing us. Being envied is nothing to be proud of, is it? It is as empty and hollow as the eighteenth pair of black shoes in the back of the closet. When you are alone drowning in debt how good is all that stuff? Our Lord warned us of the praise of men (Matthew 6:1-4).

Our quest for more stuff costs us much more than we gain. Credit card debt is counted in the tens of thousands per family among religious and non-religious people alike. The government is not the only one who cannot balance a budget. We learned well from our leaders, and our children are learning well from us.

Individuals are in debt up to their eyeballs. Homes have been lost, cars have been lost, and--worst of all--families have been lost. How much has it cost me to be envied by my "friends?" Marriages are ending in divorce, but boy we have a lot of stuff to divide up. This carnage is the result of our pursuit to find happiness in possessions. Of course, having stuff has not made us happy.

Our search for happiness has led us to another dead end. Happiness could not be found in possessions. If preachers would only preach men the Bible, they would have preached what Jesus said. "And he said to them, Take care and be on your guard against all covetousness, for one's life does not consist in the abundance of his possessions" (Luke 12:15). If life does not consist in the abundance of the things I possess, then why do I spend my life pursuing possessions? Oh, I know, that is what my preacher keeps preaching to me every week.

According to the Bible, life is not about possessions, but how many sermons emphasize getting more stuff? The lives of those who have God should be different from those who do not. The preaching of money and possessions could be done by a humanist just as well as any self-proclaimed bishop. Humanists at least admit their primary focus is the here and now but the preachers are lying and deceiving people.

More Fun Will Make You Happy

The third persistent message from the pulpits of prosperity preachers is this: Have lots of fun. This one says God wants you to be happy. I realize that if I say He does not, then I sound crazy. Let me remind you that this book is about being happy. It is not a matter of God not wanting you to be happy, he does. But where is happiness? You will not find it in the places and things you typically are being told to look.

Please note how that message also mirrors the world. Maybe it is to keep you distracted from the failure of money and possessions. So maybe we should just forget all that serious stuff. What you need, what we all need, is more fun. If you have lots of fun, you will be happy.

Like kids going to an amusement park, folks flock to the sold out arenas to see the show the preachers will put on. How can one distinguish between people of faith and people who have no faith? They seek money, we seek money. They crave things, we crave things. All they want to do is have fun, and so do we. And, like them, our lives are all about physical, temporal, carnal things. So we watch games almost every day.

We have become crazed with entertainment. Poker has become a spectator sport. Poker! Not only can we watch but we can also play with the pros. We watch them on sixty and eighty inch television screens. We interact online with competitors. Poker is not back room or back alley any more. It is front and center in every arena of life. The celebrities play poker. Certainly it cannot be anything wrong if our favorite celebrities do it.

We all want to be millionaires, and we are only one game show, one scratch on a ticket, or one poker hand away. Does that describe those who call themselves Christians or those who do not? You cannot tell the difference can you? Do Christians gamble? Of course they do, it's fun! But it is not even just about the money, it is also about the fun. We love to have fun, fun, and more fun.

Men often play more video games than children. Did you ever think that would happen? The children often have to wait for dad to finish before they can play. Of course dad can afford the games, so he gets dibs. I have actually seen video game championships advertised on television. Really! Huge numbers of grownups commit hours and hours to specialize and hone their "skills" at a video game. There are clubs and championships and a whole community of gamers. There was an air guitar championship. Read those words again, air guitar championship, wow! I could say more about that, but I will not.

Given our craze for fun, it is no wonder one of the favorite sayings of our children is, "I'm bored!" Maybe you have heard it. What do they mean? I'll tell you; they mean, "Hey, you clown, entertain me." They can barely contain themselves when their fun is temporarily suspended. Wonder where they got such a mindset? Parents are being reared by children, not the other way around.

Nothing is sacred or off limits from our turning it into fun. We are so confused and crazed for entertainment that God is even a spectacle and a circus. We do not go to worship God. We go to have church! We go to be entertained. How seriously can you take a "worship service" today? And, are you not amazed that it is taken for granted that God approves of whatever we imagine to do. It does not matter how far removed it is from anything He ever said. Most people never even ask, "Does God approve of my actions in worship?"; they just do it! Coincidentally have you ever considered if God approves of what you are doing in worship (Colossians 3:17)?

You can lift weights for Jesus. Of course you can, all of the apostles did it. You can run miles for Christ. After all, Paul was on the track team. You can have contemporary, traditional, and any other worship style you want to have, because they are all revealed in the Bible. One church marquee offered three different worship services. It was three churches in one. Apparently, Burger King is not the only place you can "have it your way." You can do whatever you want and then you can tell yourself that it is for God; but, really, it is just for fun.

This mindset is what allows one to leave a night club on Saturday, and go to church on Sunday. Where he can hear the same music, and do the same dances. Except when he goes to have church his way, he can call it praise dancing. If you choose not to praise dance, you can get "crunk for Christ." I know that is not "old King James," but I do not think that is in any modern version either; nevertheless, since it is so much fun to us, it must be acceptable to God.

You can call it praise dancing if you like, but it is the same dancing they do in the club. Done with the some of the same people for the same reasons, because it is fun! Changing the location does not change what you are doing. You can dance next to the preacher on Saturday, and everybody can dance for God on Sunday; then, God must approve, because it is so fun to us. Church is fun, and if it is not then I am not going!

This kind of attitude and atmosphere is what allows the outrageous and destructive preaching we hear today. A man is told the reason his wife does not respect him is because he does not make enough money. Man that is funny, everybody laugh. Then he is hit with this one: If he made more money, he would have gotten more respect; or maybe if he made more money, his love life at home would have been better. Wow, these are funny, is not this good preaching! Did you have a good time today at worship your way?

What is a wife to think of her husband when she leaves after hearing such a message? What is a husband to do when he leaves after hearing such a message? Please do not tell me that he is to go home and figure out a way to make more money. Please do not tell me, that she is to feel justified in her lack of respect for her husband. Instead tell me something crazy like, she did not marry him for money.

For all the women who think those things are funny and should be preached, let me ask, "What if the sermon were directed toward women?" "Honey, he would love you more if you lost more weight. The reason he does not love you is that you are too heavy." Or, "Maybe, Sweetheart, if you cleaned the house better he would speak to you more often. The reason you do not have any conversation is because the house is too messy." Wow, is that not funny!

These are the kinds of foolish and hurtful statements made by people who worship money, things, and fun, rather than God. A husband is to love his wife as Christ loved the church (Ephesians 5). Her size or the cleanliness of her house should have no bearing on his treatment of his wife. A wife is to respect her husband like the church does Christ. His wallet has no bearing on the matter. God said ". . . .let each one of you love his wife as himself, and let the wife see that she respects her husband" (Ephesians 5:33)." But you do not hear that from preachers, because that would involve preaching the Bible.

Entertainment has even made its way to funerals. People have turned funerals into festivals. Maybe it is our disdain for the sober reflection of life and death, or maybe it is our desire to be entertained that drives it. I suppose it could be a little of both. But, when people die I wish preachers would stop telling families not to cry. Jesus cried when He lost a friend (John 11:35). He never referred to His friends' death as a home-going celebration. Wonder where we got that idea? Jesus wept when his friend died, because He loved him.

If a person is not to cry at the loss of a loved one, when is anyone ever to cry? Some folks cry over the loss of their football team and then party at the death of a loved one. It does not take a genius to see that something is wrong with that. Grief should be had and felt at the loss of a loved one, not the loss of a national championship. How did you do when your team lost the last big game?

More <u>Pleasure</u> Will Make You Happy

The fourth message of prosperity preaching is this: Pleasure is what makes one happy. We have reached the point where preachers are preaching pleasure. There are no rules, from God. The only thing that is really important is that you are happy. You deserve to be happy. I understand why non-Christians say that, but preachers are now preaching the same message: "Whatever you want to do is fine; no one can judge you."

Scripture has been sterilized. God no longer judges. Christ is grace only--those who profess to be Christians sound just like the humanist and atheist. If you think it is alright, then it is alright. No wonder the world's view of morality looks just like that of religious people. Chances are good you cannot tell us apart.

To hear people who say they have faith try to say that anything is wrong would be funny--if it were not so sad. When a moral decision needs to be made, people who call themselves Christians disregard every passage of Scripture and fall over themselves to misquote and misapply the one that says you cannot judge.

Let us be clear; Matthew 7:1-5 does condemn a certain kind of judging. But just read the verses and it is clear the Lord is denouncing hypocritical judging. The person with the beam should not hypocritically judge the one with the mote. But please read the passage and turn off the preachers and the talk show hosts.

The Lord says, "First take the log out of your own eye, and then you will see clearly to take the speck out of your brother's eye." "First" and "then" are important words. Jesus does not say to leave the speck, because you have a log. He said first get the log out, then you can see clearly to get the speck. The Lord teaches we are to avoid being hypocritical in Matthew 7:1-5. In John 7:24 He tells us to judge righteous judgments.

I understand why those who profess no faith would say that no one should judge them, but there is no reason for those who profess faith in Christ to say the same things. The reason they do is their faith is as physical and carnal as those without faith. There really is no distinction.

Preachers actually tell people that God endorses homosexuality. Even people who make no claim to believe the Bible know better than that. You can argue against the inspiration of the Bible if you like. You can decide you do not believe the Bible. But nobody should so denigrate the Bible as to suggest it does not even say homosexuality is wrong.

There is not even a sliver of honesty in that! David and Jonathan were good friends, but somebody has to tell you to read homosexuality into their friendship. All the passages that do clearly condemn homosexuality are ignored, changed, or altered to "mean" something different. Romans 1 and 1 Corinthians 6:9-11 are clear: Homosexuality is fornication and all fornication is always condemned in Scripture (Ephesians 5:1-5). God's people are never to participate in Fornication. A man having sex with a woman who is not his wife is committing fornication. A man having sex with a man or a woman having sex with a woman is committing fornication.

Those who profess belief in Christ need to look long and hard into the mirror of Gods' word (James 1:22-25). Are we "Christians" of convenience or conviction? Have you changed your view of homosexuality because the world around you has said it is alright? Will you not say what the Bible says because you stand to lose friends, family or financing?

We are to speak the truth in love (Ephesians 4:15), the problem is no one will speak the truth. Celebrities, radio personalities, actors and actresses will you continue to sing God's praises on one hand and endorse homosexuality on the other? Do you really believe you can walk in light and in darkness (1 John 1:5-8)? God made a man and a woman, Jesus said this is what God did from the beginning (Matthew 19:3-9). The world says a man with a man is acceptable, what do you say? Jesus is clear, we cannot serve two masters. He is also clear that if we do not confess Him before men, He will not confess us before His Father in heaven (Matthew 10:32-33). If one believes he can endorse that which God condemns and still please God it will be a sad day at the judgment for that person, and I say that lovingly.

Unrestrained sex runs rampant in the church. If homosexuality is acceptable, surely adultery and other forms of fornication are. If the preacher is gay and can ignore those passages that condemn it, how can he preach passages that condemn adultery--or any other form of fornication? How can God be love and desire his happiness on one hand and not allow the same for others? How can heterosexual fornication be condemned? Truth demands consistency.

Here is a question for you to consider; think about this and answer as honestly as you can: How would your preacher preach or you teach, 1 Corinthians 5:1-10, which condemns heterosexual fornication? Would you agree with the apostle Paul and say that a man should not be sleeping with a woman who is not his wife? Would you and the preacher call that sin?

If you would agree with Scripture and condemn that fornication, how would he preach or you teach 1 Corinthians 6:9-11, just one chapter later, which condemns homosexual fornication? Would you suddenly reverse yourselves and say that this fornication is okay? How far have we gone when two men can have sex with each other and it be acceptable, even God approved; but a man who sleeps with a woman, or a woman with a man, before marriage is wrong. Our solution is as lamentable as the problem; instead of agreeing with God and saying all fornication is wrong, "religious" people simply agree with non-religious people and say, "Let us change the definition of marriage, and then let them continue to do what God condemns." Amazing!

Still, the message from preachers is that, the real key to happiness is pleasure. God just wants you happy, even if being happy is contrary to His word and the persons good. We are not helping people who are struggling with sin by telling them to continue doing it. There is no happiness in sin. Now the people without faith actually laugh at those who profess a belief in God. And why not, the preacher does not even believe his Book. The members do not even believe the message.

The atheist and humanist must take great delight in listening to professed preachers and Christians agree with them. Nothing is wrong unless you say it is. What about lying, stealing, cheating, drugs and adultery are they wrong only if you say they are wrong? People are hurting and the church is telling them to keep on keeping on. Sin hurts it does not make one happy.

It is popular to say we love the sinner but we hate the sin. The problem is we are telling the sinner that what he is doing is not even sin. If we love the sinner like we profess, hating the sin would involve helping them get out of sin. Instead we are encouraging them to continue in it. Our hypocrisy is sad and makes our professed religion silly. Stop following strangers on twitter and start following Jesus and the apostles!

The proof is in the pudding, or the accuracy is in the actions. That preachers and members believe pleasure is the key to happiness is evident by the lives of the religious and non-religious. We have given ourselves to unrestrained pleasure. It is as if the world and the church have conspired together to sell sex.

Check the messages you see and hear from the world and the church. The bar scenes where the guys and girls are checking each other out tell us that happiness is in pleasure. The videos with the girls, barely clothed, walking around the singer tell us happiness is in pleasure. The radio hosts who always announce the party that will shut the city down tell us happiness is in pleasure. We go to the same clubs as the world and we do the same things as the world. But we do these things and still call ourselves Christians.

The performers on the stage are "Christians." He just called women everything but women, but he is a Christian. His lyrics are all about what he is going to do with some of these same girls tonight, but he and they are all Christians. The patrons gyrating on the dance floor are "Christians." The men and women buying each other drinks at the bar are "Christians" the DJ spinning the records is a "Christian." How would this be any different if they were not? Would this scene be different if it were the world? "No worries; we will be praise dancing tomorrow. I'll meet you on the dance floor when we meet to have church!"

We are overly saturated with sex. In every area of life--on the television, in magazines, on the internet, over the radio--these all give us a steady diet of "Enjoy pleasure." Two and three-year-old children are learning the same dance moves and doing the same things as they are seeing adults doing. Our homes are in such chaos because our children are learning from us, and we are learning from church.

Can we all agree that young boys should not be looking at nude pictures of girls and women? Did you know that girls also get addicted to pornography? Children are taught how to use condoms in school. I still have a hard time understanding how that could happen, but those who profess Christ think self-restraint and abstinence are wishful thinking, so do those in the world.

The Bible teaches self-control (2 Peter 1:5-6). Instead our children are taught safe sex. You do appreciate, that you cannot teach someone to have safe sex, without teaching them to have sex. All sex before marriage is sinful sex. Why, are children of believers taught to have any sex? Could it be because there is no distinction between those professing Christ and those who make no profession? Wonder why so many politicians television personalities and preachers succumb to infidelity? Maybe it is our permissive attitude toward sex. Maybe it is because we do not believe sex before marriage is sin, or sex with another person's spouse is sinful.

We teach our children to have sex; we parade it in front of them; we sell it to them; and then wonder why we have all the troubles we have. Do we really want to teach children to have safe sex, and then have to provide them abortions because they are not ready to be parents? Could it be that they are not ready to have sex?

How many young people wish they could have their virginity back? How many wish they had waited? How many have diseases that will plague them for the rest of their lives? How many have hurt themselves and wish they could undo an abortion?

The next time you are infuriated by a report that a nation is exploiting children--that young girls and boys are being sold into prostitution and being sexually abused, take a long hard look at our nation and churches. Who stands to profit from our children's having sex? Who profits from our children's having abortions? Who profits from our children's seeing and hearing things and then mimicking them? There are many people, groups, and industries exploiting our children right here at home. I hope your home is not one of those being exploited.

So how did things get so bad? The worldly have been very crafty in how they have operated. They did not go for the children first. They went for the adults. If the adults wanted unrestrained pleasure, then the world would give it to them, telling them it would make them happy. They would be free to do anything and everything they wanted. We went for it. We bought it hook, line and sinker. And when they got us, they got our children.

It has reached the pulpit and preachers hold God's Book in one hand while telling men that God does not judge or care what man does, as long as man is happy. They know it is wrong. You know it is wrong. Our children even know it is wrong.

Let's win our children back, by first getting our act together. Let us all stand up and say that there are boundaries. It is right to say "No." Truth does exist. There are things we should and should not do. Our children need to learn these things from us. We should act a certain way and we should not act other ways (Galatians 5:19-22). But so often the church is silent on morality, because the church sold her morals for pleasure a long time ago. The only ones fooled by our hypocrisy are us.

False Preaching Based on False Promises Always Fails People

These are the reasons prosperity preaching is failing people. This kind of life does not lead to happiness. It leads to misery. People are not closer to God due to this kind of preaching; they are further away. Folks do not know God; they have never met him.

They know the god of the preacher--in fact, very often he is god to them; meanwhile, the God of the Bible, the One Who judges, corrects, and instructs, the One Who determines a man's love for Him based on that man's keeping His commandments (John 14:15; 1 John 2:1-3), is barred from church. He cannot come in. He is never allowed to speak; rather, false promises are made in His name. False cures are offered in His name.

False doctrines are taught in His name. And the world laughs and mocks while the church keeps partying. Prosperity preaching is making people miserable. It is putting more distance between the world and her Savior. This kind of preaching allows religious people to love the world (1 John 2:15-17), live like the world (James 4:1-4), and one day, sadly, religious people will be lost with the world (Matthew 7:21-23; 2 Peter 2:20-22).

If you are tired of this kind of dead-end religion, then I have great news for you. There is nothing wrong with you. I repeat there is nothing wrong with you! You have just been listening to the wrong messages and looking for happiness, in all of the wrong places. Joy, contentment, peace, and happiness, are out there. They are not myths. They exist, and you can have them. You just need to look in the right place.

Now is the time to remember the point I made before we got started. You are a spiritual being! You are a soul with a body, not a body with a soul. Your truest self is spiritual. Because you are a spiritual being, you can never find happiness in physical things. Happiness is spiritual! This is why correcting physical flaws can never solve spiritual failings. Just how much time, energy, focus and money have you spent on fixing physical things? None of it works for very long, if it works at all.

The reason is simple: No amount of money can buy relief for your spiritual pain. No amount of pleasure can make you feel better about your spiritual plight. No amount of entertainment can ease the problem of sin in your life. No home makeover or body makeover can help. What you need, what we all need, is a soul makeover. Here is both the problem and the solution:

The problem is that you cannot find happiness in anything physical. The solution is you that are not simply physical. You are a spiritual being, trying to solve spiritual problems with physical solutions. You have searched for happiness in money, possessions, entertainment, and pleasure; unfortunately, therein you will never find it.

You must start looking for spiritual keys to unlock the door to happiness. Some time ago, I read an article featuring people who had gastric-bypass surgery. There is nothing wrong with having the surgery. Some people need it and can really benefit from it. The article was interested in the ability of the people to keep the weight off. And for many people this was an unforeseen struggle. One person made a comment that I will never forget: He said, "They cut out the fat tissue, but they could not cut out what caused me to overeat in the first place." How insightful! Please read that again and think about this: You cannot solve spiritual problems with a physical scalpel.

Consider these two things as we think about our relationship with God: First, if we do not know God's Word, we can never know the Truth about God (John 8:31-32). Preaching today rarely if ever gives you God's Word. Second, God is Spirit but religion focuses on the physical. This is why so many people are disappointed and sad about their relationships with God. This is why one can say, "I have God in my life," and still be miserable.

There is no chance of finding lasting happiness by following prosperity preaching. Prosperity preaching never tells you what God said--which is recorded for us all in the Bible. Instead prosperity preachers are constantly telling you what God is saying--which is supposedly revealed only to them. They always tell you God laid something on their hearts. They tell you God told them today. They tell you, sometimes in the midst of a sermon, that the Holy Spirit just revealed such to them.

The reason you (cannot) know God's Word is because according to them they just got the latest "download" from God 30 seconds ago. Sometimes it seems to come to them mid-sentence. This takes God's Word out of your hands, and puts it solely into theirs. No other single factor will hurt your relationship with God more than to have God's Word taken from you and put into the preachers mind and mouth.

The Bible is all-sufficient (2 Timothy 3:16-17). You may not want to be dependent upon the preacher, but prosperity preaching leaves you no choice. Anytime the Bible is taken out of your hand, it makes it impossible for you to know God's Word. You can only repeat and trust the preacher's word. This dynamic does not allow you to have a relationship with God based on His Word. It creates a relationship with the preacher based on what he said God told him.

Scripture is clear that this is not God's desire for you. He inspired the apostles to write His word so that when people read it they could understand Him (Ephesians 3:4). With prosperity preaching, though, instead of reading and understanding you must come and be told. Since the preacher's latest "conversation" with God is not in your Bible you must come to him to get it. History is clear on this point. This is always bad for you, and always good for him.

You might respond by saying, my preacher uses the Bible. When they do use the Bible, which is a rare occasion, the Bible is really more of a prop than the source of Divine Truth. Ask your preacher, if you can get a conversation with him, if he believes the Bible is the all-sufficient Divine Source of Truth. Ask him if he believes the Bible is all one needs to live faithfully on earth and then go to heaven (2 Peter 1:3). Listen closely to the answer and know this. If he says "Yes," then that latest "message" he got was not from God, because if God's Word is all we need, then we did not need the preachers latest message God "laid on his heart."

However, if he says "No," then that means everyone before him did not make it, because before he was born the Bible was already here but his message was not yet. Was God's Word sufficient before his birth? Paul said it was (2 Timothy 3:15-17). If it was then those who lived without his new message were just fine. This also means you are just fine without his new message.

Prosperity preachers misquote or take passages so far out of context as to make them unrecognizable. Read the first point again and consider it. How effective and relevant is the Bible if the preacher is constantly getting new messages. This is the reason people can quote their pastor better than they can the Lord and the apostles. Why would one listen to Paul if his pastor is getting new information every Sunday?

Every time a preacher says God told him something, he lessens people's confidence in the Bible. This is one of the main reason people do not read the Bible. It also explains why folks concept of God bears no resemblance to what the Bible actually teaches about God. Sadly, far too many preachers do not believe the Bible is

God's final all-sufficient Revelation to man, and this disbelief is what they teach their members.

They have a Bible to show you, they may even reference it; however, when the Bible's Message is put next to their new revelation, the Bible becomes secondary. This makes our religion nothing more than our thoughts, and this is equal to no religion at all.

What Do You Think?

1. What are some distinctions between God's people and the world?
2. Does Christianity have any impact upon daily living? If so, in what ways and what areas?
3. What is sin, list some? Compare and explain Matthew 7:1-5 and John 7:24
4. What are three reasons we cannot find lasting happiness in physical things?
5. Discuss God's instruction on contentment 1 Timothy 6:6-9.
6. Discuss the difference between 1 Corinthians 5:1-3 and 1 Corinthians 6:9-11.
7. How do John 4:24 and Colossians 3:17 impact our worship?
8. Discuss the messages from pulpits today. Is our religion spiritual or physical?

Chapter 3

Seeking Happiness in Things

Our Feelings Follow Our Thoughts

You could feel very strongly about God, but be very wrong about God. Most people's relationship with God is faker than a three dollar bill and about as stable as a house of cards on a birds wing. As long as their lives go well, they and God are fine; however, as soon as something goes wrong in their lives, they turn against God and curse everything holy. How can folk have a relationship with God when they do not even believe God? Ask the typical person who claims a relationship with God how often he reads God's Word. I am sure the answers would surprise no one.

Put these two things together: one, preachers are not preaching God's Word; two, listeners are not reading God's Word. Given these things, how can anyone who hears such preaching have a relationship with God based on God's Word (John 17:17)?

False Beliefs + False Feelings = False Reality

The physical preaching these souls are subjected to does not build a relationship with God. It builds a kind of religious superstition. It builds a false relationship with God, based on what the preacher says about God. "Whatever my pastor, bishop, or whoever said about God is what I believe." And as we have seen, preachers say a lot of things which are not true about God. The result is a religious system that is built on false beliefs, which produce false feelings, and a false reality. Folks believe things that are not true, then their feelings follow their beliefs. So whatever they feel God is doing becomes true for them, even if what they live is not what they believe. Let me explain further.

There is a great chasm between what religious people hear and believe about God and what they live every day in their lives. If what preachers were telling you worked, then you should be happy. Your life should be one giant thrill ride. But how has your life worked out based on what they have told you God said?

Did you get all the "blessings" you were promised? Did the windows of heaven open for you? Or, are you still going to work every day? Are you still at a job you do not like? Do you even have a job? Is your home life terrific? How is your peace of mind? You never worry do you? By now you should be retired, sitting on easy street. I understand you might be tempted to defend them. You might say that we are to wait on the Lord. You might say we should just be patient. You might say God is testing you. Where did you get those kinds of ideas?

Surely they did not come from the same people making the promises did they? How convenient; I tell you God is going to give you something that never comes, and when you begin to wonder why, I tell you that you just have to keep waiting. You know some folks have died waiting. Friend, if it looks like a scam, smells like a scam, and sounds like a scam, it is a scam. Men have been scamming others in the name of religion for quite a while (Daniel 2:1-12; Acts 8:9-11; 2 Peter 2:1-3).

Remember what they told you. They told you, and continue to tell you, to sow your seed money! Give to God and he will give to you! You cannot out-give God! Some of you are robbing God! And when you tithe your money, you feel that God will open the storehouses of heaven! "The reason you do not have peace is because you are not tithing," they say! The reason you do not have joy is because you are not tithing! God is just about to do something great! Just hold on and keep waiting! Wait for the Lord! In the meantime sow your seed money!

Or they tell you this tried and true one: The reason you have not prospered yet is because it is not your season. Tell the truth; you do not know when or if your season is coming do you? Friend, let me assure you that your season is never coming. Ten years from now you will still be sowing and waiting on your season; you will still be tithing, but will not have received your blessings. I know you do have fears and doubts and that you are anxious. You do go home alone and wonder. Your life does not mirror what you are taught, and it is more than likely the case that you are not happy. This reality is detrimental to people's faith; because the life people live is so different than what preachers promise, many people have been turned off to religion in general and Christianity in particular. Sadly, they have never heard what God says. They have only heard false promises from prosperity preachers.

The Fruit of False Realities

The result of misinformation about God is that people believe what they hear actually comes from God. They believe something about God that is not true. And when what they believe is not realized, they get angry with God. Jesus told religious people who did, as they supposed, work in His name that He never knew them and they were to depart from Him (Matthew 7:21-23).

You might be one of those people. You know that what you hear preached every Sunday is not what you live Monday through Saturday. If you are one of those people, the inconsistency has probably been gnawing at you for some time. You probably just decided to suffer in silence. You sure did not want anyone where you attend to know that you were struggling with the issue of belief. How could you be spiritual and struggle with such a basic thing as belief? You may be scared. If the other members knew your thoughts they might think of you differently.

When you struggle with belief it leads to all kinds of other struggles. You begin to wonder if God loves you; I once did. I have wondered, "Does God care about me?" I have wondered whether God were aware of what was going on in my life. I have felt alone and unloved. I have sat and have sung the songs and wondered why I did not feel what everyone else was feeling. I certainly did not want anyone else to know that I was struggling with these thoughts.

It is for this reason that I believe I know how you are feeling; and this insecurity is likely the reason that you will never say "it." So please let me say "it" for you. I think if we say "it." If we get "it" outside of ourselves, we will have a better chance of dealing with this insecurity and overcoming it. Here is what I believe many believers are feeling. If they would say "it," "it" would go something like this:

> I love the Lord. I am trying to live faithfully. The problem is, the things I am being promised are not happening in my life. I do not know what is going on. I feel unsure about my relationship with God. I often wonder if I am pleasing Him. I struggle to do the right things. I often feel spiritually empty. I sometimes feel like I am just going through the motions. I do not like my life. I wish it could be different. I feel like God is very far from me. I have no one I can talk to about this.

David could relate. He felt abandoned; he felt like a worm; he felt like no one cared for his soul (Psalm 22). God's prophets asked more than once why the wicked flourished while the righteous perished. Habakkuk wondered if God were being just in using Babylon to judge Israel (Habakkuk 1:12-13).

You may be feeling this way about your relationship with God for a variety of reasons. The false, unrealized promises of preachers will make you feel this way; because prosperity preaching provides nothing substantial, there are a lot of fancy saying, music, singing, and entertainment but nothing lasting, helpful, or practical for your life. Maybe, life has caused you to feel this way. Maybe you got hurt. Your life was going along great. You loved God and Jesus, and felt great about the relationship. You attended services and did good things in your community. Then tragedy struck your life in an unspeakable way. The thing or person you held most dear was taken away. So you turned to the only one you could, God. But He did not answer. He did not help. You called, but He did not seem to hear. You cried and He did not deliver. You kept praying and everything remained silent. Over time you began to wonder, does He care? Is He real? Why bother?

Or maybe you got here because choices made by other people have caused great hurt in your life. Some Christians have found out that their spouses were cheating. It is difficult to imagine the pain and betrayal one feels when his spouse cheats on him. Some Christians have learned that their precious babies are now strung out on drugs. Some have found out that their daughters are pregnant. Do Christians get abortions? Some Christians are dealing with their children's announcing that they are homosexual. These things are happening in the lives of believers. The people who hear the sermons every Sunday are dealing with these things through the week.

Sometimes we arrive at this place because of our own decisions. I have spoken to men and women who feel trapped in their marriages. They know God says that marriage is for life; this is also the vow they made to each other, but now for any number of reasons they want out. The thing that is said most frequently is that they feel trapped. It is amazing what the word trapped does to our minds.

But they are not trapped; they are in the same relationships they volunteered to enter; however, when they begin to feel trapped, they want the first thing any trapped person wants: Freedom. But because they are Christians they do not divorce. Instead of divorcing, they spend their days pining away and lamenting their desperate and dire circumstances--never realizing they are not trapped, they only feel trapped. Do you feel you are you in such a situation from which you cannot escape?

I do not mean to minimize people's feeling. What people feel is real to them, even if what they feel is not actually real. Just here I need to take a brief trip with you to discuss feelings.

Feelings Follow Thoughts

Feelings are not like a math equation. People seem to believe that if a certain set of circumstances exists then they must feel a certain way based on the given data.

In other words, their feelings naturally follow the equation. I know people act this way, but it is completely wrong. Just because a certain thing happens, it does not mean one must feel a certain way about it. Man is in control of his feelings. Feelings are not some strange mysterious thing over which one has no control (1 Peter 2:21-25).

Our feelings are the result of our thoughts. We think first, and then we feel what we think. Genesis 37 is a good example of how one's feelings follow his thoughts. Jacob was the son of Isaac who was the son of Abraham. Jacob had 12 sons; one of his sons was named Joseph. Joseph was Jacob's favorite. As a result of Jacob's favoritism, Joseph's brothers hated him (Genesis 37:4).

Jacob sent Joseph to check on his brothers as they worked away from home. As Joseph approached them, their hatred was put into action. They talked among themselves about how they would kill him. There was some disagreement among the brothers: Some thought to kill him, but others wanted to save him. Eventually, they decided against killing him, and opted to sell him into slavery, which they did. It is what they did next that helps us understand how man's thoughts precede his feelings (Genesis 37:31-36).

The boys were deceptive and dishonest. They did not say an evil beast killed Joseph, but they wanted Jacob to think that, which is why they dipped Joseph's coat in blood. For a moment, do not focus on the boys; rather, focus on Jacob. When Jacob saw the coat, he formed a thought in his mind. He announced that thought in the words "a fierce animal has devoured Joseph." He believed Joseph had been torn into pieces. To emphasize his certainty, he said his conclusion was not doubtful. It was certain in his mind that Joseph was dead.

His feelings naturally followed his thoughts. What would a loving father do, believing his favorite son had been violently killed by a wild animal? He cried, mourned, and grieved. He felt so bad about his loss that he thought he would die grieving his son, but we know that Jacob did not. Joseph was not dead. He was alive and would one day rise to second in command in Egypt.

Please do not miss the point: Jacob's feelings naturally followed evidence. He saw the coat. He concluded Joseph was dead. He grieved the loss of his son. Because Jacob thought Joseph was dead, he felt loss--even though in reality Joseph was not dead. No one would say Jacob did not feel grief, pain, hurt, or loss; however, all would acknowledge that even though his feelings were real, they were not based on something that was real. This is what we all need to understand about our lives and our relationships with God.

Suppose a lady married a man because of what she saw in him while they were dating: He was gainfully employed, he wore a suit to work every day, he led a religious group at his church; and even though she was not "in love" with him (whatever that really means) she married him anyway.

Suppose then that after the marriage he quit his job, and he stopped working every day, opting rather to pursue his own business ventures. Do you think she might be upset? She would probably feel like she was not getting what she had signed up for. She might even feel trapped in her own marriage.

Whom should she blame? Should she blame anyone? She had wanted to do the right thing, she had taken her vow very seriously, she had married for life, but look at what happened to her. We might say she should blame her husband. He does seem to be the most obvious target. After all he is the one who changed, right? Maybe she should blame herself. Were there any red flags? If she had ignored things, why had she done that? Maybe it was her parents fault. They should have told her more about men. All of these targets would be suitable when looking for someone to blame. If there were any blame to give out, it could be shared a little by all: her husband, herself, and her parents.

I would submit to you, though, that ultimately the One to receive the blame would be God. You might disagree; she probably would also; however, if not overtly, we might all do this subconsciously. We need someone to blame, so we place blame at the feet of the one who is in charge--who is more in charge than God? It was God who had made the rule that she had to get married to have sex anyway. God is the one who had made the rule that she was to stay married once she had been married. He is the One holding her in this terrible trap. If he were not responsible, then who would be? What one does next is likely not planned. If God be doing something to someone that that one does not like, then that one likely will not do something for God that He would like. The tendency is to conclude that since God is doing this to "me," I will do something to Him.

So man makes up his own mind; he concludes, "I will keep coming to worship. I will sing songs of praise. I will pray, give and commune." He then stops actively participating when God starts talking. It is not until the preacher starts preaching that God is even allowed to speak; and when God speaks, He tells that man what He wants that man to do. At this point the trouble begins.

Man does not say it out loud, but he says it by his life. The message to God is "No. No, I will not do what you are saying." Imagine the wife in the example at hand hearing a sermon from God's Word on how she is to submit to her husband (1 Peter 3:1-7). She will listen, but she will not live it. By her life she is telling God, "Since you will not listen to me, I will not listen to you."

She might as well say, "God I keep telling you that I feel trapped. I keep telling you that I want to get out of this marriage, but you will not listen to me. Instead you keep holding me here in this trap, and then you have the nerve to tell me to submit to this man? I have news for you God. You will not listen to me, so I will not believe you." In the end, the preacher is preaching to a "believer" who really does not believe.

Consider another case, a man spoke to me when he was contemplating getting married. I told him he should not marry this particular woman. I had my reasons. The bottom line was that I did not think it would work out between the two of them, and I told him that. Sadly, this scenario has happened on more than one occasion. He is my friend. If one has a friend, and that friend is about to marry someone he does not believe he should, does he tell him? Well, I do not know about you, but I do. Knowing people like I do, I know that we are all capable of doing great con-jobs on ourselves. The more we want something, the less likely we are to be the best sources of objectivity. If the subject is something as serious as marriage, please talk to a friend who can be objective and honest with you.

This man heard not only my counsel, but others said the same thing. He married her anyway. Not long after the marriage, they began to have trouble. They tried to work it out, but to no avail. Eventually, the marriage ended in divorce. He was a wreck. He could not believe this had happened to him. Do you think he spent anytime wondering where God was in this whole process? Do you think he ever wondered why God would allow such a thing to happen? His heart was broken, and where was God?

I have talked to many people in a multitude of circumstances. I have spoken with husbands who no longer want their wives, and wives who no longer want their husbands. I have spoken with people who are divorced and want their spouses back, but the spouses do not want them back. I have spoken to children who do not like their parents, and parents who are not at all thrilled with their children. I have spoken to people who have suffered the loss of children, parents, and siblings.

In nearly every instance, someone sees his once peaceful life turned upside down. Everything he had held dear was ripped away. His belief in God was challenged. His faith was tried and I am sad to say, far too often the person is giving up. He is not giving up on himself. He is not giving up on life. He is not giving up on his career. I am sad to say that they are giving up on God.

As a rule, men cannot see how God could allow whatever tragedy they are experiencing to happen to them. It is amazing, really. It is like having a bad day at work and coming home and yelling at your wife, or it is like having a neighbor destroying your flowers and then turning and kicking the dog. All should know, when one person does you wrong, you do not take it out on someone else. People are giving up on God, although God has not done anything to them. He has not harmed them in anyway. He has not withdrawn himself from them. He is still fully engaged in the relationship He started with them and only wants what is best for them.

Sadly, people are hurt by someone or something else, and in response turn on God. This thought is often heard: "If God were good, why did He not stop it?" Since He did not stop it, they cannot believe He is good any more. Their thought process is simple, "If God loved me, He would have protected me." Many folks in the pews are broken. In their minds, their lives are shattered, and very often they become despondent and quit believing in God.

They are so shaken by the circumstances of their lives that they become jaded, hardened, and suspicious. Instead of the challenges to faith providing endurance and strength, these challenges of faith produce the exact opposite. These people just stop believing God. They do not stop believing God exists; rather, they stop believing anything God says.

Whatever God says begins to fall on deaf ears. One of the oft used phrases by people who are in this place is, "I know the Bible says but..." This is an acknowledgment that the source of the message is God; however, such a response really says, "I do not believe It." The result is a life that acknowledges God, but does not walk with God. There is no joy, no comfort, and no peace because in their minds, God has failed them.

If this person were asked to identify his problem, he would list all of the things he believes hinder his life. If the problem is his marriage, then his spouse is the problem. If the problem is in his home, then his children are the problem. He might even list the problem as a co-worker, money, health, or some other thing.

Though these things are significant, and for some troubling, they are not the problem. The problem this person is experiencing is his relationship with God. What he is going through is the common circumstance of every person's life. No person is an island, and no one has suffered in a way that is wholly new to humanity. If you are in this predicament, be assured that someone, somewhere is going through what you are going through right now; some would even argue that what they are going through is worse than what you are going through.

So what a person may identify as the problem is not the problem. The problem is his relationship with God. The ironic thing is that the solution to the issues of life is God. One's relationship with God should serve as the foundation on which to build a house that will stand when life's storms come.

"It is not you, it is me" is an oft used break up line. It is used as relationships are coming to an end. It is usually among the last things said. What may have been a once great relationship has met a very sad end. The way people talk about God, one would think God was the problem. Friend, I do not believe it; I do not believe it for one second. I do not want anyone's relationship with God to ever end.

Maybe you are unhappy in your relationship with God. Maybe you believe God has failed you in some way. Maybe you feel He should have done something that He did not do, or maybe you think he should have provided for you, protected you, or helped you; but he did not. Now, you sit in misery every Sunday and hear His Word preached. You have given God all that He is going to get from you, and you are about to break it off. Before you do, I need you to understand something very important; I need you to know unequivocally and absolutely: It is not God--it is you!

Maybe the leading cause for your problem is your misplaced expectations of the relationship in the first place.

One cannot have a good relationship with God if that relationship is not based on His Word. Jesus prayed, "Sanctify them through your truth, your word is truth" (John 17:17). He also told those who believed on Him that if they continued in His Word, then they were his disciples and they would know the Truth and the Truth would make them free (John 8:31-32). Have you ever read the Bible through for yourself?

What Do You Think?

1. Would you say you are listening to God?
2. Are relationships with God based on God's Word or the "Pastor's" word?
3. Do you know anyone who has given up on God?
4. Can you relate to David's feeling of abandonment? (discuss Psalm 22 and what you can do)
5. What do people mean when they say, "I know the Bible says, but ..."? What are the implications of this statement?
6. Can we control our feelings, or are they automatic responses to certain data?
7. Discuss Jacob's feelings being real but based on false information (Genesis 37). What if you believe something about God that is untrue?
8. Discuss John 8:31-32 and John 17:17. What is the basis for your relationship with God?

Chapter 4

Misplacing Expectations of God

"God's Word is the Basis of Our Relationship with Him"

How would God say your relationship with Him is going? Read the question: I am not asking how you would say it is going; rather, how would God say it is going. If He were to answer, His Word would be the basis for His answer. God will not keep promises that He never made, and the only promises He has made are found in His Word. How would you feel if people demanded that you keep promises that you never made? If you would not be agreeable with it, then make sure you are not doing that to God.

Our relationship with God must be based on Truth (John 8:31-32). His Word is His revealed Truth (John 17:17). Our relationship with God must also be based on Scriptural, spiritual expectations. Lots of relationships with God end in trouble because they begin in trouble. The individuals coming to God just do not know it, for they neither know nor understand His will. This almost happened to a man named Naaman. His relationship with God almost ended before it began because what he expected from God was not done by God.

Naaman was the captain of the Syrian Army. He is described as a great man, he was mighty of valor. He led Syria to victory over Israel. Through their conquest, Syria took some Israelites captive. As great as Naaman was, he was also a leper. Leprosy was an incurable disease that if it was able to run its course would result in slow, painful, and certain death.

A young maid from Israel told him that he should go see the prophet in Israel, for he could help Naaman with his leprosy. After some missteps, eventually Naaman came to the prophet. Naaman came with great pomp and circumstance. He stood before the tent of the prophet and waited to be healed. The prophet sent a messenger with simple instructions to go wash in the Jordan River. This was not what Naaman expected. And when he was not healed the way he thought he would be, he got angry. "But Naaman was angry and went away saying, 'Behold, I thought that he would surely come out to me and stand and call upon the name of the LORD his God, and wave his hand over the place and cure the leper'" (2 Kings 5:9-11).

This is absolutely amazing. You must stop and consider it. Here is a man with an incurable disease. Naaman is going to die. He is told how to be cured; however, he is willing to keep his leprosy and go home and die with it because he is angry about the instructions the prophet has given him to be cleansed. The reason for his anger is this: He thought it would be different, and his expectations were not met! Let us not go forward until we spend some more time thinking about that. The man left the tent in anger, with his leprosy. Death was more desirable than his expectations going unmet. Can you imagine it?

Do You Suffer From Naaman Syndrome?

If you can, will you try to also imagine what this must look like from God's perspective? Far too many people have Naaman syndrome when it comes to God today. People come to God--not as suffering, sorrowful, sinners--but believing they are pretty good; they are just in need of a little tune-up.

We are in sin! We will die and be lost eternally! Though we are lost, we do not like the way God told us to be cleansed. The result is that we attempt to start a relationship with God while having the wrong attitude and misplaced expectations. We come to God to negotiate with Him, not to submit to Him. We come to tell God how our relationships with Him will be. We do not ask God what the terms of the relationship are; rather, we set the terms.

There are many reasons for this. One is the Mount Everest-sized pride that rules our hearts. Whatever happened to "Speak Lord thy servant hears"? Or, "You are the potter and I am the clay"? Or "Here am I, send me"? Or, "Not my will, but your will be done"? Remember when people used to fear the LORD. They had reverence for God. They did not dare to do anything that belittled Him. The fear of the Lord is still the beginning of wisdom (Proverbs 1:7). People walk around like they have a chip on their shoulders with God. I mean no disrespect, but it is almost as if they are saying if, "I see God, He had better watch out. He knows I am mad."

Pride is the result of people's not realizing how bad sin is. Did you know that it would have been just--that is, fair--for God to have killed Adam and Eve when they took the first bite of the fruit (Genesis 2:15-17)? Death would have been a fair verdict. And if they had died in sin, of necessity they would have gone to hell eternally, "For the wages of sin is death, but the free gift of God is eternal life in Christ Jesus our Lord" (Romans 6:23).

This would have been right and proper for God to do. Have you thought about that with your sin? If you have committed one sin, it would be right for God to kill you, and for you to live eternally in hell. But He did not (John 3:16). God's grace and mercy should curb all of our pride.

Another thing that we need to appreciate is what it cost God to forgive our sin. God is so holy and sin so awful that it took a perfect sacrifice to satisfy the justice due it. God gave Himself, His only begotten Son for our sin. A sober reading of Isaiah 53 should humble us to the point of tears. We could do nothing for ourselves. God laid His only Son on an altar and sacrificed Him for our sins. Where is the place for our thoughts, or anger, at the terms He has set to have us back?

Amazingly, the thought that God could and would set terms is lost on people. God's Word is so infrequently read that many have set their own terms. Even when the subject of pardon for sin is broached, people ignore plain Bible teaching, opting for their own versions of pardon. Like Naaman, they have their own thoughts. It would amaze many if they were to open their own Bibles and read (James 2:24). The way preachers preach, one would think the Bible said the exact opposite of what it says. The verse reads, "You see that a person is justified by works and not by faith alone." Did you know the Bible does not teach faith only? I know someone will go and grab a host of passages where the Bible teaches the necessity of belief and say that I am wrong. Without writing a different book, let me say this: You are right, belief is essential (John 3:16-19; 8:24); however, that in no way diminishes or removes the words of James. My point is simply that you hear every week that you are saved by faith alone, while at the same time the Bible expressly says this is not the case. While faith is essential (Romans 5:1), it is not faith only that saves. Did you ask God about the terms of your relationship with Him, or did you set them?

Did you know that you are also saved by grace (Ephesians 2:8-10)? Grace and faith are two things; therefore, it cannot be faith only. God's works save; man's works do not (John 6:28-29). We are also saved by Christ (Philippians 3:20). We are also saved by God (1 Timothy 1:1). And this will blow you away: The Bible also says that baptism saves us (1 Peter 3:21). If you want to see a preacher tap dance, listen to him attempt to explain that away. People determine what behavior is acceptable in their relationship with God before they ever enter it. They do not say this out loud to God, but this is how they approach him. Like Naaman, they have their thoughts.

Let me throw another one at you: Did you know that we are not to tithe today? I know, to hear your preacher tell it, you would think you could read it on every page of the New Testament, but you cannot. One of the great failings of this physical preaching is that it scams you out of your money, and builds a false relationship with God.

If you are professing to be a Christian, you should not be tithing. Let me explain. The Bible says because the priesthood is changed, the law must be changed (Hebrews 7:12-15). The text is about Christ's priesthood compared with Aaron's priesthood. The reason this is important is the priesthood is connected with the law or covenant. For instance Aaron's priesthood is connected to Moses' Law. In order to be a priest under the Law of Moses you had to be from the tribe of Levi (Numbers 3 and 18).

Our Lord Jesus could not be a priest under the Law of Moses because he was not from the tribe of Levi (Hebrews 7:14), but Jesus must be a priest upon His throne (Zechariah 6:12-13); therefore, in order for our Lord to be our High Priest and make atonement for our sins he had to change the law. Thus our Lord brought a new covenant (Matthew 26:26-28). He changed the Old Testament Levitical priesthood. And by so doing it became necessary for him to change the Old Testament Law. So why do preachers keep telling you to tithe per the Law of Moses? The tithe was for the Levites for their service (Numbers 18:21-24). The way preachers preach tithing you would think tithing was part of the Lord's New Covenant. It is not! You cannot have Christ as your High Priest and have Moses as your Law giver (Hebrews 4:14-16).

This is why Christ came to fulfill the law and take it out of the way (Colossians 2:14). He took away the first so he could establish the second (Hebrews 8:8-13). Listening to some preachers, you are never told that; they find a way to make these passages teach the priesthood is changed, and the laws referring to sacrificing animals have changed, but the law of tithing? Well, that one remains forever--of course it does. Works great for them, but it is not so good for you. The words of our Lord are chilling: "Let them alone they be blind leaders of the blind and if the blind lead the blind both will fall into the ditch" (Matthew 15:14). Friend, listening to these preachers is like being led by a blind man, in the dark with your eyes closed across a balance beam over the Grand Canyon. Both of you are going to fall into the ditch. They have Bibles, but when you see their Bibles, think props not preaching.

It is not hard to observe that relationships with God are not founded on Truth, because when what people expect from God does not happen, they complain very loudly about God. They behave as if they had an agreement with someone and he did not uphold his end of the bargain. They walk around angry, acting as if God has let them down. They cry "Foul" to God, to life, and to whomever will listen. Does this describe your relationship with God? Some folks come to worship angry at God, worship God in anger, and leave upset that they did not get anything out of the worship.

What are Your Expectations of God?

Have you ever asked yourself what you expected from God in your relationship? Or have you always assumed that whatever you wanted from God would happen? Maybe you have been listening to preachers instead of reading your Bible. I want a job, so God will give me one. I want a house, so God will give me one. I want a child, so God will give me one. And once He gives me what I want, nothing had better ever go wrong with it. My job must always be pleasant. My house must not decay, burn, or fall down. My child must always be safe, secure, and healthy. Is this the deal that you made with God?

Maybe this kind of idea comes from a misunderstanding of a statement Job made. It would probably surprise many to learn that Job was wrong about the cause of his suffering. He had a great disposition in his suffering, but he did not have all the information. After Job lost his children and almost all of his possessions:

> Then Job rose up, and rent his garments, and having shaven his head, fell down upon the ground, and worshipped, And said: Naked came I out of my mother's womb, and naked shall I return thither: the Lord gave, and the Lord hath taken away: as it hath pleased the Lord, so is it done: blessed be the name of the Lord. (Job 1:20-21)

What most people do not know is that Job is wrong. He has a great attitude about his suffering, but he is dead wrong about who is causing it. In reality, most people have taken his thoughts as true when they are not. A simple reading of Job chapter one would show that while God did give Job's blessings, He did not take them away.

God allowed Satan to take those things from Job, but God did not do it. Job did not know about the conversation in chapter one between God and Satan. It happened in heaven. Read the book of Job, and you will see that God never explained Himself to Job; rather, He asked Job some questions that he could not answer (Job 38-42).

It will surprise some to learn that the book of Job is not even about Job. Like the rest of the Bible, it is about God. Satan is accusing God of being unjust for allowing Job, a man who has sinned, to live (Romans 6:23). He also accuses God of not being worthy of respect and faithful obedience. He alleges that God has to buy faithfulness. He says God has hedged Job in, or protected him from harm, and that this is why Job is serving Him. Now, sadly, the religion of today would agree with Satan.

Preachers are saying, "Give to God, and He will give to you. God will bless you." As a result, when life happens, people say what Job said: "God gave it and God took it away. God is testing me or trying me or attempting to teach me something." This idea is absolutely wrong. God is defending His holiness and faithfulness

(Romans 3:23-25; James 5:10-12). The thing that Job held most dear was not his possessions or even his children. What he held most dear was his relationship with God, but God was no longer talking to Job. Throughout the book, Job's greatest lamentation is "God will not answer me. In reality, the book was never about Job; it was always about God.

The last time I checked, the potter did not owe the coffee cup an explanation for not making it into a vase. The way folks talk about God, they sound like they control Him. When we are young, we sing, "He's got the whole world in His hands," but when we are old, we live like we have Him in our pockets. This is the result of the physical, carnal preaching that we hear every week. It is so much about us that God had better not let us down. After all, we gave our money; He had better uphold His end of the deal.

We might deny it, but our words, clichés, and expressions about God reveal our expectations of Him. Some folks refer to God as "the man upstairs" and other similar foolish things. If God is a man, then what is the point of our trusting and worshiping Him? Scriptures states the exact opposite of such nonsense. God is not a man (Numbers 23:19). Sadly, one day men will find out. "These things you have done, and I have been silent you thought that I was one like yourself. But now I rebuke you and lay the charge before you" (Psalm 50:21).

God is not like us. He is not a man. He does not lie. He does not make mistakes. He is not our personal assistant. Our arrogance toward God is further evidenced when we encounter trouble. When some who profess belief in God have problems, they say things like "I'll just turn it over to God." What do they mean by that?

Turning It Over to God

When I was young, my brothers and I would try to get each other into trouble. One way (there were many) we did that was to act as translator for the other whenever we said anything. Usually it was a conversation in which we did not want someone to know our actual thoughts. Maybe it was a dish we did not like. We might be asked how we liked it. Not wanting to be rude or hurt the host's feelings we might give a vague non-de-script answer (hoping it would be sufficient without going into further detail). If one of us heard this, that one would say, "Now, let me tell you what he really means." Knowing each other as well as we did, the translator was usually right; we just did not want the host to know it.

In that vein, let me translate the phrase "I'll just turn it over to God" for you. What this really means is this: "I have encountered a situation in my life that I do not want to deal with. I do not have any desire or will to ascertain how I got into this pickle. Neither am I interested in figuring out whether or not it was my fault or someone else's. However, I keep God on a leash for just such occasions. And now I will call Him and tell Him to fix it, so I can get back to some of the more important things in life--one of which is to keep making decisions like the one that got me into this jam in the first place."

The beauty of this little gem is that it works on everyone and everything. It is like a great sponge: It cleans up everything. You can turn your neighbors, children, father, husband, wife, sister, brother, postmen, mechanic, and everyone over to God. But wait, there is more. You can also turn your job, car, house, and everything over to God. You just call Him up, and He will take care of it. Really, God is like the cleaners and you are just dropping off your dirty laundry. Just turn it over to God and you can keep it moving. After all, did you and God not make this deal? Do not stop and deal with it--just turn it over to God. Do not accept responsibility for causing it--just turn it over to God. Do not ever ask, "Is it me," even though often times, you and everyone else know it is--just turn it over to God. If you are wrong, do not ever apologize--just turn it over to God. Do not worry about other people--just turn them over to God. Do not live your life--just turn it over to God.

We should cast all of our cares upon God (1 Peter 5:7), but this idea of turning something over to God without working to solve situations is wrong. You are not in a relationship with a god. You are trying to be in a relationship with the Almighty God. Who do you think you are? God is not your doorman waiting on you to drop off your rain coat and umbrella. Casting our care implies our need for Him.

Turning something over to God suggests that He is waiting to serve you. What is the nature of your relationship with God? If you have turned something or someone over to God, maybe you need to go back, get it back, and deal with it yourself. Chances are good He has already told you how to solve the situation in His Word.

Are you having trouble with friends, family, bosses, employees, children, or spouses? If so have you read Ephesians?

Chapter four tells us to walk worthy of the calling of God because we have been redeemed by the blood of Jesus, and bought by the purpose of God. We should change our attitudes and behavior. We should walk after Christ and the new man He has created (Ephesians 4:17-23). Chapter five teaches us about Christ and His church, using marriage as the means of that message. Chapter six teaches us about children and how parents, fathers in particular, should behave toward them. In this relationship with God, are you listening to God or are you just turning things over to Him?

Just Pray About It

Another expression people use that reveals their expectation of God is this: "I am just going to pray about it." May I translate please? When a person says, "I am just going to pray about it"; largely he means just that. It will take another book to talk about prayer, but let me say this about the phrase "I am just going to pray about it." When people say it, they mean it. All they are willing to do about whatever difficulty they are having is pray about it. The totality of their willingness to deal with, work on, grow in, or get past the thing that troubles them is limited to prayer. Here is a question to consider: Has anyone ever taught them how to pray? The apostles thought enough of the Lord's prayer life to ask Him to teach them how to pray. Have you ever asked to be taught how to pray? The only times some pray are at meal time, bed time, and trouble time. Which time is your time? Do you just call God when things go wrong or when you want something? How do you feel about people who try to have this kind of relationship with you?

Others hold prayer as the one true indication that they are living right. You should read Matthew 6, because these people have not. They talk to God all day, every day and they make sure that when you are around you hear it. They humbly tell you what a great prayer life they have. They really believe they will be heard for talking a lot. When they pray, usually they are turning somebody over to God. They talk a lot but say nothing; worse still, they do not dare live what they pray.

There is one important point about prayer that you need to know: If you pray to God about something, God expects you to do something. Read the prayers in the Bible. You will work hard to find the person praying in Scripture who did not do something about that for which he had prayed.

Nehemiah prayed for his nation. His prayer is recorded in the first chapter of his book (Nehemiah 1:4-6). The rest of chapter one Nehemiah continued his prayer confessing sin and pleading to God for forgiveness. He pled to God based on the Word God had spoken to Moses. That if his people sinned, they would be driven out of the land, but if they returned God would forgive and restore them back to the land.

After his prayer Nehemiah resumed his normal activities as the king's cupbearer. One day he was sad in the king's presence and the king asked him what was wrong. In chapter two of Nehemiah, the book records the conversation he had with the king. Listen to a piece of that conversation. "Then the king said to me, 'What are you requesting?' So I prayed to the God of heaven. And I said to the king, '. . . if your servant has found favor in your sight, that you send me to Judah, to the city of my father's graves, that I may rebuild it'" (Nehemiah 2:4-5).

Notice what he said. He prayed to God. He asked the king to send him to Judah so that he could rebuild it. I strongly encourage you to read the rest of the book of Nehemiah and see what he and his nation went through to build Jerusalem's wall. God was with them, but it was because they were with God. They did not just pray about it. Nehemiah went to Jerusalem, he surveyed the situation. He secured the help of the people; together they withstood adversity and they all set out and built the wall. Nehemiah 4:6 says, "So we built the wall, And all the wall was joined together to half its height, for the people had a mind to build." This is a great example of making prayer effectual.

Listen More Than Talk

Prayer is man talking to God. God wants us to pray to Him. He has promised to hear and answer our prayers (1 John 5:14-15). If prayer is man's talking to God, the Bible is God's talking to man. Which is more important? Which is better for us to know? I might be the only preacher who says this to you, but I say it because it is true. Friend you would probably do yourself better if you prayed less and read your Bible more. It is very likely that God has already answered your prayer in His Word. You need to know the One to

Whom you are praying, and the only way to know God is to know His Word.

Before your next prayer, please understand this: Prayer is not designed to take the place of Scripture. It is amazing that we want God to listen to us, while at the same time we have no desire to listen to Him. How often do people reject, neglect, or ignore what God said in His Word, then pray to God and demand to be heard? Let me give you an example of what I mean.

Many people are having troubles in their marriages. They often go to God in prayer for help and deliverance. Many have been loosed by preachers, but not by God. Folks are always assured that God is with them no matter what they do, but what if God has said something about marriage? What if God said that we are to behave a certain way in our marriages? Do you suppose it is okay to ignore what God said, do things our own way, and then--when it does not work out--pray to Him for help?

Note Peter's words to husbands about how to treat their wives, and consider the connection to God's Word and prayer. "Likewise, husbands, live with your wives in an understanding way, showing honor to the woman as the weaker vessel, since they are heirs with you of the grace of life, so that your prayers may not be hindered" (I Peter 3:7).

Have you ever thought about that? God says to treat your wife right; he says to honor her, and you respond, "No. I will treat her any way that I want to. She is my wife, and I will tell her where to go and what to do. I will tell her when to go and what to wear. I will tell her how she should sit, sleep, and speak. This is my house and she is my wife. I run this!"

Now, when that same attitude and disposition runs into trouble--I cannot imagine how or why--but when trouble comes, what do we do? We pray, of course. We tell God to fix the problem. We plead really hard for God to solve our issues. We insist that if He loved us, He would move on our behalf. We cannot imagine His not doing it, and we wonder why He has not yet. Maybe it is our pride, maybe we have some strange expectations of our relationship, or maybe we have never read 1 Peter 3:7.

We are to learn our wives and live with them based on that understanding. Husbands are to honor their wives. Does your wife feel honored? Any husband, who refuses to honor his wife, should stop praying to God for help. Instead, he should read God's Word and obey It. He should let God tell him, and he should stop telling God. Here is a great example of when it is appropriate to stop praying and start reading, understanding, and obeying God's Word.

This example also has application to wives. The same context speaks to wives and tells them how to treat their husbands (1 Peter 3:1-6). God tells wives to submit to their husbands. Submission is a dirty word to many people. It is really unfortunate, but it speaks to a greater reality. When the Bible is misunderstood, lives cannot be lived correctly. Some wives who also call themselves Christians refuse to submit to their own husbands. Choosing rather to have an attitude that says, "I am not listening to some man." They may even say to their husbands, "I wish you would try to tell me what to do." Many husbands know that their wives' mothers, sisters, brothers, fathers, cousins, dogs, rats, and cats come first--and then them; if the husbands do not like it, the wives might say, "He knows what will happen. It will be a cold day followed by a colder night." Some go so far as to say things like, "I cannot trust any man and I will not submit to one." I have heard of women who have the word "obey" taken out of their vows.

Chances are good this attitude will run into trouble. In the end this woman--if she is married--has a husband; she sleeps with him or given this kind of spirit maybe not anymore. We could go around and around talking about each other. We could all share horror stories of how bad men and women are, but it would not do us any good. The point is this: To wives, God said, "Submit," and to husbands, God said, "Honor." In another place, God told wives to reverence their husbands, and husbands to love their wives. In order to have a good relationship with God, all must learn His Word and follow It. No one can be successful with God while rejecting what God tells him to do to have a relationship with him. If you are not submitting to your husband, stop praying to God to change him, and start obeying God. God says that we are not to allow the sun to set on our anger. Do you fight and go to bed angry?

Peter says that how we act toward each other, impacts our prayer life to God. The idea of "hindered" in 1 Peter 3:7, is that our prayers will be cut off. It is a warning from God. Given the fact that prayers can be cut off, it makes you wonder how many prayers actually reach heaven. Maybe we never got the answers we wanted because our requests never made it to heaven. Do we realize that

God has said this? Do we know that there are terms and conditions to our prayer lives, do we care?

A few verses later Peter says, "For the eyes of the Lord are on the righteous and his ears are open to their prayer. But the face of the Lord is against them that do evil" (1 Peter 3:12). The righteous whom Peter has in mind in verse 12 are composed of those who follow the instructions in the first 11 verses. The righteous are those who hear and do what God says. Their prayers are not hindered, and God hears and answers them.

Fathers Talk and Sons Obey

It is a serious mistake to believe that we can have a relationship with God, without knowing or listening to God. We are His children, and He is our Father. Children are to respect and obey their fathers. What do you think of the following? A child comes to his father and says dad I am ready for my allowance (Now we could go into how, if the boy is getting an allowance, he is way ahead of the game. After all, even without the allowance he has a roof over his head. He has food to eat. He has a place to sleep and clothes to wear. In other words, he should already be thankful for what he has been given, before he ever considers asking for anything else. He has all of that and his father has been gracious enough to give him an allowance.).

He approaches his father and asks, "Dad, I would like to have my allowance."

His father looks at him and says, "Son, you know I love you. And it is my joy to give you an allowance. I am actually thankful that we are in a position to be able to give you one, but, Son, you are asking for your allowance but you did not do any of your chores."

The son looks his father in the face and says, "Yes, Dad, I know, and I did not want to say this to you, but I am not going to do my chores; however, I still want my allowance."

The father, stunned by his son's response, thinks about all that he has given him: the house he provides for his son, the food, clothes, video games and everything else. He has always done so much for his son. He thinks about how the chores are not that difficult. He also thinks about how the chores would actually only help his son later in life, of how doing them would build character and instill discipline in his son. He thinks about the allowance his son is requesting, and how ungrateful his son is being.

Then, in an amazing turn, the father says, "Alright, Son, since you want it, here is your allowance." He reaches into his wallet and pulls out the money to hand it to his son, but just before he hands it to him he says something incredible: "Son, you do not have to do what I ask, but I will do everything that you ask. You can reject my word, but I will listen to yours. You can take and take and never give."

What would you think of a parent who did this with his child? Would you say that would be absurd? If so, I would certainly agree. I know of no parent who has taken this approach with his child, but what is even more amazing is that God's children try to take this approach with Him. How much more absurd it is for us to pray to God and demand that He move for us, while refusing to do what he commands us to do!

Like the father, God has already given so much to us, the children. Our first response to Him should be to fall on our knees in constant praise and thanksgiving for what He has already done. He created us in His image. He gave us the freedom to choose. He provided the world, and all that we have to use in it. Ultimately, He laid his only begotten Son on the cross for us. Regrettably, we spend little time praising God and thanking Him for what He has already done. Instead, like this spoiled rotten, unthankful child, we constantly ask for more, while at the same time, refusing to do what He says to us in His Word? God says, "Honor your wife"; but we say, "No." God says, "Submit to your husband"; but we say, "No." God says, "Do not provoke your children to anger"; but we do it anyway. God says, "If you and your brother have problems, go to him and solve them"; but we say, "No, we will talk to everyone else but our brother." How many times has God said something to you and you said, "No"; then you have gone to Him wanting Him to listen to you and to immediately do what you have asked? Again, may I suggest that you stop praying and start reading, studying, learning and meditating upon God's Word!

The Word of God is God's talking to man; prayer is man's talking to God. Do we listen to God? Do we do what He says? Do we even read It? Well, do not worry about it. Maybe God will open the treasure houses in heaven, and--just before He gives us our request--like the father in the story he will tell us, "Do not worry.

You do not have to do what I say, but I will do everything that you say. Just pray about it."

What are Your Expectations of God?

Who is in control--you or God? We act as if we control God and when He does not respond the way we think He should, we are disappointed; accordingly, as with any relationship in which expectations are unmet, problems follow. Unmet expectations may be among the greatest disappointments in life. If you have ever expected something and it did not happen, then you know how devastating unmet expectations can be. Relationships can end when expectations go unmet. Our relationships with God can end as well if our expectations from God go unmet.

The question that we need to answer is this: Are our expectations of God based on anything He has said? It may surprise you to learn that many of the sermons you hear do not have their origins in the Bible. Often, preachers are telling you what they think or believe God will do; they are not telling you what God said He will do. And if the preacher should use a verse from the Bible, he is taking it so far out of context that by the time he is done its intended and original meaning is unrecognizable. As a result, your expectations are based on what the preacher said, and not what God said. You cannot hold God accountable for misinformation about Him. Let me give you a quick example of what I mean.

In Genesis 6 a command is given to build an ark. Why have you not built one? You mean your preacher has not told you that God is going to flood the world, and you need to build an ark? You might say God said that to Noah, and that would be true. You might also say that God said that to Noah for a specific reason, and that would also be true; therefore, you do not have to build an ark. Why, then, do I hear preachers take Genesis 12, just six chapters later and tell you that God made you promises. In Genesis 12 God made some promises; why, then, are you told to expect the fulfillment of these promises? Your answers about the promises should be the same as they were about the ark: They were specific promises to Abram.

God promised Abram that he would give him land, a nation, and a seed. He promised Abram that his seed would bless the whole world. Why would a preacher take this specific promise to Abraham and tell you that you are going to receive the same things

Abraham did? You should no more expect to have what Abraham had, than you should feel compelled to build an ark.

The promise to Abraham had a spiritual component to it. The seed that was promised is Christ (Galatians 3:16). Through His death, burial, and resurrection, Christ has blessed all nations. There is nothing about this promise that you should take and make physical to you; however, preachers will tell you that you are an heir of Abraham and that you should reap his blessings. The blessings are spiritual, not physical; that is, salvation, not riches. Paul explains:

> For as many of you as were baptized into Christ have put on Christ. There is neither Jew nor Greek, there is neither slave nor free, there is no male and female, for you are all one in Christ Jesus. And if you are Christ's then you are Abraham's offspring, heirs according to promise. (Galatians 3:27-29)

The entire book of Galatians is about the Gospel that brings salvation. Through Christ, all nations are blessed with forgiveness of sins. Pertaining to salvation, everyone is equal in Christ. This is the promise God made to Abraham; however, some preacher has told you that being an heir to Abraham entitles you to physical riches like Abraham enjoyed. And now your entire relationship and expectation of God is centered on God's blessing you with wealth because Abraham was rich.

Care should be given to note how seamlessly some preachers move from the misapplication of the promises to how Abraham paid tithes. Of course, then they tell you that if you expect blessings from God you must pay your tithes to God. You should counter with the fact that God made the promises before Abraham paid the tithes, not the other way around. The point is this: God cannot and will not be held accountable for a preacher's misinformation about Him. You must stop allowing people to tell you what God said and read and study for yourself, because when what you believe does not happen, you will be disappointed with God.

What Do You Think?

1. What will God use as the basis for one's relationship with Him?
2. Can Christ be a priest under the Law of Moses?
3. If Christ changed the priesthood, what else must change? Should men tithe under the Law of Christ?
4. Is one saved by faith alone (James 2:24)? What else saves?
5. How do misplaced expectations affect one's relationship with God?
6. Is there a time when one should not pray?
7. Does God have requirements for one's relationship with Him?
8. What is the reasonableness of one's asking God to provide for him in prayer while refusing to do what God says in His Word?

Chapter 5

Viewing Blessedness from a Spiritual Perspective

"Without God Our Happiness can be Taken"

Having discussed why physical religion fails, in this section we turn our attention back toward God. God is Spirit (John 4:24). His Word is Spirit (John 6:63). Jesus came to give spiritual life (John 10:10). We are made in God's likeness, thus we are spirit (Genesis 1:26-27). Our focus needs to be spiritual. Let us put away our desire for physical things to define our spiritual relationship with God. Let us get back to thinking spiritually about our God and ourselves.

How often have you asked someone how he was doing and the response was, "I am blessed"? People respond this way because they are taught to, but because of the truths in the first four chapters likely, it is not true. It is not true, because the preaching they hear and believe does not lead one to be blessed. The next time someone responds that way, ask them why they are blessed? It will startle them, but listen closely to the response. What you will hear is something physical: "I have my health" or "God has really blessed me." Maybe they will note their jobs or things or something similar. Christians are blessed, but why?

What It Means to be "Blessed"

This is not what it means to be blessed. Being blessed in Scripture is spiritual not physical. God uses the word "blessed" in both the Old and New Testaments of His Word. The word "blessed" means "happy." Please note that this describes the person--not something he receives, but something he is. Scripture tells us the person is happy, and it tells us why he is happy. Read Psalm 1, it describes what we all want to be. It shows us a happy man. The man is happy because of what he does, and what he avoids. Note the happiness is spiritual.

Psalm 1 – The way the blessed man lives

The first description in Psalm 1 is of the man's way of living. His life is put into motion. It is described in terms of a progression of life. The first word is walk. This man is happy because he does not walk in the counsel of the ungodly. From cover to cover the Bible tells God's people not to live like the world. You will never be what God wants you to be if you live out of harmony with what God has revealed. Happiness is a spiritual walk. We should not believe and practice what those who do not believe in God believe and practice. Blessed is the man who does not walk in the counsel of the ungodly.

Also, happiness is connected to the messages one receives and believes. This man does not receive and order his life from wicked counsel. To be wicked is to be ungodly or irreverent, that is. It is descriptive of one who is impious. The ungodly person does not respect God (Psalm 10); instead, he argues against God. He does not believe God (Psalm 14:1). He does not listen to God. Happiness begins with the right attitude toward God, an attitude that acknowledges that God is superior to man, not the other way around.

How many people are calling themselves Christians though they receive their messages and beliefs from those who oppose God? For example, it is understandable that the world says you cannot judge. You must never tell anyone that anything is wrong. Since, according to non-believers, there is no objective standard of Truth that governs life, no one has a right to tell another person something that he is doing wrong. Those who believe in God should not say such things, for if one does believe in God and His Word, then he will believe that God's is the standard by which morality is measured. For this reason, it is terribly wrong for people of faith to take Matthew 7:1-5 and apply it to all judging. When the text is so clearly condemning hypocritical judging. If you read

Matthew 7:1-5, you will see that even in the verses the Lord said, "First cast out the beam ... and then you will see clearly to cast out the mote." The Lord does not want the mote to stay, He just wants the beam out first. Were it not for accepting the counsel of the ungodly, people of faith would never echo such things (cf John 7:24).

The blessed man does not walk in the counsel of the ungodly; he does not stand in their circles; he does not sit in their communities. The progression begins with walking and ends with sitting. This is the sad reality of many who begin with God and end cursing God. They begin to walk among those who have no regard for God. They walk among them, they stand with them, finally they sit among them. The sad cycle now complete, they themselves become scornful mockers of God. How many people claim to be blessed by God and act with scorn toward what God says? How many people "of faith" read Genesis 1, but parrot the words of an avowed atheist? Believers have gotten their counsel from atheist so they do not believe the word was created in six days. How would they explain Exodus 20:9-11? It is one thing for an atheist to believe in evolution, but how would one explain "Christians'" denouncing Genesis 1? Do you get your advice from people who oppose God? The blessed man does not.

There is no lasting joy in mocking our maker. If there is no God, there is no happiness, for there is no future for which to hope. There is no present to enjoy and no past to remember delightfully. If we will die and that is the end, we are miserable (1 Corinthians 15:19). Let us eat drink and be temporally merry for tomorrow we die. Men may argue against it, but the fact remains the same. This is why happiness is not under the sun; it is beyond the sun. You cannot be happy listening to and believing the counsel of the ungodly.

Psalm 1 – The focus of the blessed man's life

The second description is also of the man's life. He delights, or takes pleasure, in God's Word. He contemplates it and mulls it over in his mind day and night. How does this make one happy? The Word of God reveals God. When we read It, we learn Him. What we learn is His eternal nature. There is great comfort in knowing God and in knowing that He made us in His image. Thanks to God, we know how we got here (Genesis 1:26-27).

Which is more comforting? Knowing that you are the result of a benevolent, loving God Who shared His image with you, or believing that purposeless, mindless, matter accidentally resulted in you. Because God made us, we know what we are to do here, and we know where we are going when we leave here. Without His Word we could never know these things.

God's Word tells us of His grand creation (Genesis 1-2). It tells how He made us in His image (Genesis 1:26-27). Self-esteem comes from knowing that we possess God's likeness. God's Word tells of His goodness and graciousness in sending Jesus to die for our sins (John 3:16). God's Word tells us about heaven (Acts 1:9-11). It tells us how to live on earth, and how to please and worship God (Matthew 22:37-40).

God's Word is an ocean of knowledge, and we have a teaspoon with which to empty it. This is why the man is blessed who meditates in it day and night. There is so much to learn; there is so much to know. One can easily spend his lifetime reading, studying, and meditating in God's Word. This man is blessed or happy because of what he does and what he does not do.

How can people of faith be happy in God if they never read God's Word? How awful is it that the Bible is ridiculed in church! How often do you read it and meditate in it? Today if you want to insult someone, call him a Bible believer, or call him a fundamentalist, or, if you prefer slang, call him a Bible thumper. We have become so smart that these are insults to avoid. And "believers" shutter at the thought of someone ever saying this of them. How amazing is it that here is a passage that says the man is happy who meditates in God's Word day and night, but we cast the Word down and party instead. If happiness is in God's Word, then we all need to get into God's Word, and get God's Word into us. Friend it is just that simple.

Psalm 1 – The fruit of the blessed man's life

The third description is not really a description; rather, it is the result of man's first two descriptions. It is the result of the blessed man's godly disposition and his meditation upon God's Word. He will be like a tree that is planted. When we plant trees we do several things. We clear the land and cultivate the soil. We dig a hole in the ground. We plant the tree and water it. All of this describes purposeful action with proper expectation built-in. This is the way the blessed man is described. This is the natural result of his life because of those whom he avoids, and the thing in which he delights. God's Word gives knowledge and understanding. Through It we can understand God, ourselves, and our fellow man. Through It we can learn about sin, sacrifice, and salvation. This man's life is ordered by God's counsel. He interacts with his fellow man based on God's Teaching and Instruction. He thinks of himself how God thinks of him.

The man understands that since God made the world, God knows how best to live in his world. He knows that since God made man, he would know best how to interact with man. This man is like a tree that has been planted. He fears God and this makes him wise, for, "The fear of the Lord is the beginning of knowledge; fools despise wisdom and instruction" (Proverbs 1:7).

The tree is not simply planted. Note the location of the tree. It is planted by rivers of water. The man is blessed because of the preparation he takes in his life, but that preparation is nourished by a sufficient steady supply of water. The Word of God is to his spiritual life what water is to the tree. Water sustains and nourishes the tree. The tree then is able to grow, blossom, and flourish. Such is the result of the man's life. He is nourished, grows, and blooms as a result of meditation in God's Word. God's Word is living water for one's soul (John 4:7-14).

The expectation of a tree planted by rivers of water would naturally follow: We would expect the tree to grow. It does. So does the man. He is blessed because he brings forth good fruit. The reason is simple: He lives his life based on the instruction he received from God. When one takes God's Word and lives it in his life, he brings forth good fruit. This is as proper an expectation as growing is for a tree planted by rivers of water. This is why we cannot be people of faith while living like people in the world.

Blessedness is Spiritual, not Physical

Some may see in this thought that if one lives for God, then God will bless his life and whatever he does will succeed; so the preaching and teaching goes today. "Give to God, and He will give to you. Sow your seed, and God will pour you out a blessing." This conception of prosperity preaching is so opposed to God and contrary to Truth that it is hard to imagine anything worse. It is a complete and utter misrepresentation of God, Christ, and the Holy Spirit.

It is wholly against the apostle's teaching, and it is utterly foreign to Christianity. Those who preach it should be ashamed. They know they are wrong, and one day they will have to stand before God and be sentenced for their ungodly, covetous, greedy deeds; therefore, they are in need of your constant prayers that they will cease and desist before they meet God. Coincidentally, before the economic down-turn in 2008 you probably did not know that heaven's blessings fluctuated with the Dow Jones Index. Heaven's heating bill must have come due, because God closed the windows of heaven when the down-turn happened. The recession must have hit heaven as well as earth. This passage does not teach what those who see material gifts in every spiritual passage say it means.

What then is the thought behind the man's leaf not withering and whatever he does prospering. As the old preachers used to say, "I'm glad you asked." For starters, always stay in the verse and stay with the analogy and never push the analogies in Scripture too far. The comparison is between the man and a tree. He is like a tree planted by the rivers of water. What happens to trees planted by the river when the seasons change?

These trees, like others, give way to the seasons. The leaves first change to the beautiful fall colors of yellow, orange, and red. Then when winter comes the water turns to ice and the leaves fall off the tree. The point is simply that the normal circumstances of life happen to this tree as well.

Such is the case with the man. It is not a blanket statement that everything he does will certainly succeed. He does not turn into Midas because he was planted by the rivers. The statement is reminiscent of one Jesus made during his first sermon.

He told those who would listen that if they would hear His Word and do it, then He would compare them to a wise man who built his house upon the rock. He also compared those who would not hear His Word and do it to a foolish man. The latter was foolish because he built his house upon sand (Matthew 7:24-27). Here is the important piece. The rain fell, the floods came and the wind beat upon both houses. This is what those who follow the Lord must learn. The Lord never promised that the wise man's house would be immune from the storm if he built it upon the rock, but, sadly this is what those who profess belief in Christ are taught.

What He promised was that if one built his house upon the rock, then his house would stand when the storm came--not if the storm came, but when. So it is for the blessed man. He will prosper. His leaf will not fail. He will go forward. Life will happen, storms will come; however, he will not fail, because the perpetual source of his happiness is God. No matter what happens to him, nothing can move his source of happiness, because the source of his happiness is spiritual not physical; it is eternal not temporal.

Ungodliness = Un-blessedness

Unlike the blessed man, the ungodly are not so--read "the ungodly" as those who are irreverent toward God. To understand ungodliness think about it this way: What comes to mind when you hear the word "inhumane"? It is to treat a human being with less regard than is due him. We have cruelty to animal laws for the same reason. As a society, we believe there is a certain regard that is due animals; to treat them with less regard than is due them is punishable by law.

This basic concept is what is involved in one's being ungodly. Ungodliness is treating God with less regard than is due Him. It goes without saying that the regard due God excels that due animals; moreover, it is also the case that the regard due God is much higher than that due humans.

This is the reason God uses governors and other officials to teach his people about respecting him. We treat those in positions of authority with the respect due them. How would you dress and behave if you were to have an audience with the President (Malachi 1:7-8)? How much more should we regard God?

For instance, it is ungodly to take God's name in vain. Using God's name lightly, with no regard is to be ungodly. How many people have no regard for how they use God's name! So many that today His name has become an epithet and a trite expression. We should regard God so highly that we are even cautious and reverent in using His name.

Take that thought back to Psalm 1. The end of the ungodly is anything but happiness. Those that are ungodly have no substance; they have no staying power; they have no anchor. The blessed man is like the tree planted by the water. The ungodly are like the chaff. The chaff was that which flew off the wheat when it was threshed: The wheat stayed and the chaff fell to the ground or was carried away by the wind. A simple wind passing by would catch the light chaff and blow it away. Such is the state of the ungodly. This sounds very much like the state of the foolish man who built his house upon the sand. The storm came and his house fell. His house, or life, had no foundation. He had nothing substantive with which to withstand the storm.

There is no happiness in ungodliness. Neither is there any substance. Nothing endures in ungodliness, for one is left to himself. He becomes his own source of strength. He becomes his own source of knowledge. He becomes his own authority and moral compass. So where does he find happiness? He will seek out things, possessions, pleasure, and money. Since none of them can bring lasting happiness he will end where he began: Searching. Unfortunately, if he never learns better, he will spend his whole life looking for happiness, only to end his search empty-handed.

Happiness is outside of you because it is rooted in God; happiness is inside of you only because you can take God's Word and live It in your life. You are responsible for taking God's Word and applying It to your life. No one can live a righteous godly life for you, no one can make you happy, no one can give you happiness, because you take you everywhere you go; therefore, it is never the place that makes you happy. You are either happy or not before you ever get to the place. The godly are happy; It is the ungodly who are unhappy

The blessed man in Psalm 1 did not receive a blessing. The Psalm says he is blessed. This is what happiness is. God is the source and because you are His and He is yours, you are happy. This is not about how life treats you. Remember the sun shines on the good and on the evil; the rain falls on the just and the unjust alike (Matthew 5:45). The storms of life beat on everyone's house.

The difference depends upon what we are in spite of all of these things. The tree planted by the river buds again in spring. The blessed man is happy in good times and bad. The outward circumstances of life have no impact on his happiness. The reason is that his happiness is not based on anything that can be touched by the troubles of life.

Another great passage about a man who is happy is Psalm 32:1-2: "Blessed is the one whose transgression is forgiven whose sin is covered. Blessed is the man against whom the LORD counts no iniquity. And in whose spirit there is no deceit." This man is blessed or happy because his transgression is forgiven, his sin is covered; that is, the Lord counts him justified. His heart is honest and pure. This is a happy man. This state of being in which he lives cannot be challenged. A storm can take away his house, car, and clothes, yet he is still happy. He does not want the storm to destroy his life, but he knows if he lives in the world that storms happen; however, since his happiness is in God he is happy in the storm. He knows storms can take away things, but they cannot take away sin; neither can they take away the joy of having one's sins removed.

Since God is the source of his happiness, nothing can take that happiness from him. He is blessed because he is forgiven. His condition of forgiveness is what makes him happy. It provides him the basis for behaving righteously, no matter what happens in his life. Even if he should lose his health, he can be happy. Obviously, no one wants to be sick, and like anyone, if this man had a choice in being sick or not, he would choose not to be sick; but he is not blessed because he is healthy. He is blessed because he is forgiven. So what is he if he loses his health? Blessed!

True Blessedness Endures in Trial

The problem with life is that most often we do not have a choice in being sick, so we must deal with the challenges of life whether we want to or not. Sometimes the disease and sickness is terminal, and if your health was the source of your happiness, then when it goes so does your happiness. This is one of those places where people get angry and sever their ties with God. "He should not have let me get sick," they think. "If He loved me, He would have protected me," they think. "Since I am sick, God must not love me anymore."

Of course people get sick everyday all over the world. It is the common lot of all men (1 Corinthians 10:13). These facts are often ignored when we are hurting. Note the source of the man's happiness: He is not happy because he has his health; he is happy because he is righteous before God. He is happy because God forgave him. This fact is still true even if he is sick. This fact is true even if he is terminal, and far too many people who profess to believe in God miss this.

Religious people who believe God brought the sickness are wrong. Religious people who believe they can avoid bad things happening by simply not claiming them are wrong. Cancer does not care if you claim it. It happens to good people and bad people alike. It happens to old and young, righteous and unrighteous, and it has never left anyone alone because it was not claimed. Cancer is not something that is put into the lost and found and had only by those who claim it.

This is the trouble with believing what people have said rather than believing what God has said. Read Psalm 32:1-2 again. Why is this man blessed? His transgression is forgiven. If your sins are forgiven, then you are blessed. His sin is covered. If the blood of Jesus covers your sins, then you are blessed. If you are not forgiven, that spiritual state is the problem, not your poor health.

If God does not hold you guilty anymore, then you are blessed. If you are pure in your heart toward God and man, then you are blessed. For those who enjoy this state of being, nothing done to them on earth can ever take it away. Neither can any disaster impact their relationships with God. So in peace or adversity, they can be happy. In wealth or in poverty, they can be happy. This is the fundamental difference between physical religion and spiritual religion: Physical religion focuses on man and things he has; spiritual religion focuses on God and what He has done in Christ.

Do you remember when Paul and Silas were thrown into jail for preaching Jesus? It is recorded for us in Acts 16. They were imprisoned falsely and were jailed without trial. Their freedom was taken, though neither of them had done anything wrong. Here is a part of what happened:

> The crowd joined in attacking them, and the magistrates tore the garments off them and gave orders to beat them with rods. And when they had afflicted many blows upon them, they threw them into prison, ordering the jailer to keep them safely. Having received this order, he put them into the inner prison and fastened their feet in the stocks. (Acts 16:22-24)

If this had happened to you, how would you react? What did Paul and Silas do? What was their state? What was their condition? If you listen closely, you will hear an amazing thing. "About midnight Paul and Silas were praying and singing hymns to God, and the prisoners were listening to them" (Acts 16:25). This is what it means to be blessed. This is what it means to be happy according to Scripture.

Did they want to go to jail? No! Were they thrilled that this happened? No! What they were is blessed. Of the things that happened to them, nothing changed their relationships with God! In prison, were their transgressions still forgiven? After being beaten, were their sins still covered? Once they were locked up, were they still righteous before God? Were their hearts and minds pure toward God and man? If you answered "yes" to these questions, then you understand why one is blessed and where happiness lives. When the jail was opened by an earthquake, they did not escape; neither did the other inmates. They stayed, and eventually taught their jailer the Gospel and saved him and his family.

That example of Paul and Silas is not just filler in your Bible. It was the application of lessons they had learned from the Savior. Our Lord went through the storm of Gethsemane. Because He did, He was able to triumph at Calvary. He did and left us an example that we might do the same. It is said of our Lord that He endured the cross and despised the shame for the joy that was set before Him, and we are exhorted to follow His example (Hebrews 12:1-3).

I once read Acts 16:25 and focused on the words, "and the prisoners were listening to them." This prompted my thinking about others' listening to us. When the storms of life come, what do you say? Better yet, what do others hear you say? Are you aware that your adversity is a great opportunity to show and teach someone about Jesus? The other prisoners were listening to Paul and Silas sing. Do you think they would have heard them curse the name of God and the Roman government as well?

Paul wrote a letter from prison. He wrote it to a congregation in Philippi. It is called Philippians. In this letter he spoke about being in prison. His statement about his outlook while being in prison is evidence that Paul understood what it means to be happy. He told his readers that the things that happened to him had turned out favorably. He looked at them as being positive for three reasons. One, his going to prison advanced the Gospel. Two, by going to prison he preached in the palace and many heard the Gospel. Three, by his actions and reactions his brethren were strengthened. They spoke God's Word boldly without fear (Philippians 1:12-14).

Paul is a great example of a blessed, or happy, man. He lived it and nothing the world did to him could take it away. Later in the letter he told people who were not in prison to, "Rejoice in the Lord always; again I will say Rejoice" (Philippians 4:4). The prisoner was telling the free to be happy. Rejoice in the Lord. Here is where happiness lives, at last you have found it!

Each of us needs to examine his religion. Is our religion godly? To be godly is to be reverent, respectful of God. This means trusting God's Word and doing what He says (Hebrews 11). Or does my "faith" sound just like the practice of the ungodly? Do you live anyway you see fit? Do you champion the causes of the world and meditate day and night in their words or do you meditate day and night in God's? Are your morals, ethics, and view of Scripture the same as those of the ungodly? Happy is the man who is respectful of God and follows His Word.

What Do You Think?

1. What two passages cited spoke of being blessed?
2. What three things are said of the blessed man in Psalm 1?
3. What does it mean to be ungodly?
4. Why are the ungodly not truly happy?
5. Discuss the difference between physical religion and spiritual religion?
6. How can a blessed man be happy even if he is sick or terminal?
7. What does the phrase "his leaf will not wither, and everything he does prospers" mean?
8. What do Paul' and Silas' actions and attitudes in prison teach us?

Chapter 6

Understanding the Purpose of Jesus' Coming

"If Jesus Did not Come to do His Will, Then we Can't Live to do Ours?"

Why Did Jesus Come to Earth, Anyway?

If you thought differently about this question, it would change your life. It would change your view of Scripture, the Lord's work, your expectations of God and yourself. "Why did my Savior come to earth?" is a question from a beautiful hymn we sing. The answer given in the song is probably the most popular of all answers: "Because he loved me so." It is a great answer and a great song, but the answer is wrong. Love sent Jesus to earth, about that there is no doubt; however, while this explains God's motivation, it does not explain Christ's purpose in coming. The question is "Why did my Savior come to earth?", not "What sent my Savior to earth?" Therefore, the most straight forward and accurate answer to the question is this: Christ came to earth to die!

Some might argue that Jesus accomplished many things by His coming, and that would be true, and the accomplishments are all important. Among them is the fact that Christ fulfilled the scriptures (Luke 24:44). "Then he said to them, These are my words that I spoke to you while I was still with you, that everything written about me in the Law of Moses and the Prophets and the Psalms must be fulfilled." He showed us the Father (John 14:9). "Have I been with you so long, and you still do not know me

Philip? Whoever has seen me has seen the Father, How can you say, 'Show us the Father?'" He left us a perfect example (1 Peter 2:21). "For to this you have been called, because Christ also suffered for you, leaving you an example, so that you might follow in his steps."

While the Lord accomplished all of these things and more, what He accomplished only further establishes why He came. All of these things were accomplished because He came to die. We must embrace and wrap our minds around the fact that Jesus came to earth for one reason and that was to die.

Hebrews 10:5-7 says it well, "Consequently, when Christ came into the world, he said, Sacrifices and offerings you have not desired, but a body have you prepared for me; in burnt offerings and sin offerings you have taken no pleasure. Then I said, Behold, I have come to do your will, O God, as it is written of me in the scroll of the book."

He came to do His Father's Will; in order to do that, He needed a body. Hebrews 10 says a body was prepared for Him. Paul wrote, "But when the fulness of time had come, God sent forth his Son, born of woman, born under the law, to redeem those who were under the law, so that we might receive adoption as sons" (Galatians 4:4).

Jesus said He was here to do the Will of the Father and to finish His work (John 4:34). The disciples pled with Him to eat. Note His response, "Jesus said to them, My food is to do the will of him who sent me and to accomplish his work." When we know what the Father's Will and work was, then we know why Jesus was here.

The Father's Will was that Jesus die on the cross. And this was the work Jesus came to accomplish. We know this to be the case, because Jesus said so Himself. Prior to his death, Jesus was in a garden called Gethsemane praying to God. He prayed three times, and each time He prayed the same words. His prayer and statement about God show us that his death on the cross was God's Will. "Then he said to them, My soul is very sorrowful, even to death; remain here, and watch with me." And going a little farther he fell on his face and prayed, saying, "My Father, if it be possible, let this cup pass from me; nevertheless, not as I will, but as you will" (Matthew 26:38-39).

When He finished this prayer He returned to the three disciples that He had brought with Him. When we He reached them, He found them asleep. This saddened the Lord, and He asked them if they could not have stayed awake with Him while He prayed. He left them and, "Again, for the second time, he went away and prayed, "My Father, if this cannot pass unless I drink it, your will be done" (Matthew 26:42).

When He came back, His disciples were sleep again. He left them and went and away and prayed a third time saying the same words. Remember in John four when He was asked if anyone had brought Him food that His response was, "My food is to do the will of him who sent me and to finish his work." In the garden He said, "If this cup cannot pass, your will be done." The cup was His death, it was God's Will and it could not pass. He came to drink of it, in dying, to accomplish the Will of the Father.

Whatever the Lord was meaning in the garden when He asked that if it be possible let this cup pass, should not be thought of as a plea to get out of his impending death. Later in the garden, Peter cut off one of the servant's ears to protect Jesus. Pay close attention to the Lord's response to Peter: "Then Jesus said to him, Put your sword back into its place. . . But how then should the Scriptures be fulfilled, that it must be so?" (Matthew 26:52-54).

The Lord said he could ask for more than twelve legions of angels, and the Father would send them at once. He obviously was not asking for that when he prayed earlier. It is also helpful to remember that the Lord told the apostles that He was going to die before He went through the garden. He was teaching them a lesson about service and humility (Matthew 20:25-28). Without his death, the Scriptures could not be fulfilled. He had to die. This is why He came.

There is no wonder, then, that after His resurrection He charged his apostles to go into the whole world and preach the good news of His death, burial, and resurrection (Mark 16:15-16). The first time the apostles preached the Gospel is recorded in Acts 2. Matthew, Mark, Luke, and John record the events of the death, burial, and resurrection of Christ. Acts records the apostles' and disciples' spreading that message to the world. There are many parts to the first sermon the apostles preached. Prophecy is cited many times for proof and verification of the message. Joel and David were two prophets whose prophecies were fulfilled.

Signs were used by the apostles. They were eye-witnesses of the message they preached. In this sermon, note Peter's statement about God and about Christ's coming:

> Men of Israel, hear these words: Jesus of Nazareth, a man attested to you by God with mighty works and wonders and signs that God did through him in your midst, as you yourselves know- this Jesus, delivered up according to the definite plan and foreknowledge of God, you crucified and killed by the hands of lawless men. God raised him up, loosing the pangs of death, because it was not possible for him to be held by it. (Acts 2:22-24)

The Will of God was that Jesus die on the cross for the sins of the world. This is the reason Jesus came to earth. God could not die, so a body was prepared for Him. This is the work Jesus came to finish accordingly, on the cross Jesus said, "It is finished" (John 19:30). If the question be "Why did my Savior come to earth?", then the answer is that He came to earth to die, to be buried, and to rise from the dead.

That means there are a myriad of reasons Jesus did not come to earth. If you will fix this firmly in your mind it will change your life. Jesus came to earth to die for the sins of the world. If you do not understand this, your relationship with God will start out wrong and never correct itself. You will attempt to live for God expecting things of God that He never promised. There are many reasons Jesus did not come to earth, why did you think He came?

Jesus did not come to earth to stop people from mistreating others

Sometimes people make choices that hurt and injure other people. This is the result of God's creating men as free moral beings (Genesis 1:26-27). We can choose our actions, and sometimes we choose to hurt other people. This happened before Jesus came to earth. Cain killed Abel (Genesis 4). It happened when Jesus was on the earth. Judas betrayed the Lord for thirty pieces of silver. And it continues to happen today. Someone has or will hurt you. This continues to happen, even though Jesus came to earth, because Jesus did not come to stop men from mistreating one another; He came to die. If this is your expectation of God you will be sorely disappointed.

It is a grave mistake to believe that if I obey God, then people will treat me right. God never promised anyone that if you will follow Him, no one will ever mistreat you. Amazingly, in His first public address, Jesus told all who would follow Him the exact opposite:

> Blessed are those who are persecuted for righteousness' sake, for theirs is the kingdom of heaven. Blessed are you when others revile you and persecute you and utter all kinds of evil against you falsely on my account. Rejoice and be glad, for your reward is great in heaven, for so they persecuted the prophets who were before you. (Matthew 5:10-12)

It seems that those who profess to be disciples have forgotten the Words of the Master. The disciples did suffer persecution. Please note the word "blessed" in the passages, it is our word "happy." This is incredible: Jesus told His disciples that they would be happy if they were persecuted for righteousness. This has been corrupted to the point that men feel that you are blessed if you have no trouble at all. God never promised that.

The New Testament is written to congregations and individuals. The letters are full of warnings and exhortations about suffering. If we listed every passage, the list itself would take up a book. But notice just a couple of more: "Indeed, all who desire to live a godly life in Christ Jesus will be persecuted" (2 Timothy 3:12), "But if when you do suffer for it, you endure--this is a gracious thing in the sight of God" (1 Peter 2:20).

How many disciples of Jesus remember that they were called to follow His example? We are to walk in His steps. The context of walking in His steps is one of suffering and how to respond to it. Contrary to the modern thought of no harm ever happening in life, we find the opposite. If we live godly, we will suffer, and we will be happy for it. Christ suffered, and we are called to walk in His footsteps. We must all remember that the servant is not greater than his Master, nor is a messenger greater than the one who sent him. If the Lord suffered for righteousness, we should not think it strange if we do the same.

Jesus did not come to earth to stop people from mistreating you; rather, He said if you follow Him, be certain that they will. One reason is the difference between light and darkness. What will your friends say when they are ready to go out Saturday and dance, drink, and gyrate on the floor, yet you refuse to go with them because of your relationship with God. If you choose God, you will lose some friends

Jesus Did Not Come to Settle Personal Disputes

He made that clear to a man who approached Him about an issue he had with his brother. Someone in the crowd said to Him, "Teacher, tell my brother to divide the inheritance with me." But Jesus said to him, "Man, who made me a judge or arbitrator over you?" And Jesus said to the crowd, "Take care and be on your guard against all covetousness, for one's life does not consist in the abundance of his possessions" (Luke 12:13-15).

Why did they need Jesus to settle the issue? The Lord's answer reveals their problem. One or both of the men were greedy. They could have been fair and divided the inheritance evenly. The Lord's answer is telling. "Who made me a judge over you?" Jesus did not come to earth to settle estates. He came to die for the sins of the world. We are charged with fairness and equity.

To further expose the real problem the Lord followed his refusal to divide their inheritance with a parable and a warning (Luke 12:16-21). The issue was greed. Jesus charges us with dealing with our own heart issues. We must not be covetous and we need to remember we cannot fool the Lord. Instead of being greedy, Jesus taught His disciples to be content. Soldiers also asked him, "And we, what shall we do? And he said to them, Do not extort money from anyone by threats or by false accusation, and be content with your wages" (Luke 2:14).

Jesus did not come to earth to settle personal disputes. He came to die, and by His life we are to learn contentment and practice it in our own lives. If brothers are at odds with one another, they are to go to one another alone (Matthew 5:22-24). They are to do so humbly, with each one considering himself (Galatians 6:-1-5). They are not to pray, they are not to turn it over to Jesus. They are not to ask God for help. They are to do what the Lord said.

Jesus Did Not Come to Solve Social Problems

At issue is not how we treat one another. Neither is the issue whether or not the Gospel can change society. The Gospel can change us, and we can change how we treat one another. But even that is not the issue. At issue is why did Jesus come to earth? He did not come to earth to solve social problems.

Jesus was born under Roman rule. Luke 3:1-2 tells us that when Jesus was born Tiberius was Caesar and when He died that Pontius Pilate was governor of Judea. We are also told that Herod, Philip and Lysanias were rulers of the local area in His lifetime. This means that Jesus was born, lived, died and ascended back to heaven under Roman rule. If it were God's Will that Jesus come to earth to fix all social problems, then it would seem natural that He would have started by delivering His own people from bondage. But He did not.

Racial issues were a huge issue in the time of Jesus. Men hated each other and the Lord did not fix every person's personal problem. He met a woman from Samaria. He spoke to her about her life and the salvation He could give her. He used the image of water to teach her the Good News. She drew water physically, but it ran out and she thirsted again; however, He had water for her soul that if she drank would leave her never to thirst again.

His meeting with this woman from Samara was a success. She learned He was the Messiah. She believed and went and told others from her village and they also believed; it was what she said to Him early in the conversation that gives us insight into the racial issue of their day.

"A women from Samaria came to draw water. Jesus said to her, Give me a drink (For his disciples had gone away into the city to buy food). The Samaritan woman said to him, "'How is it that you, a Jew, ask for a drink from me, a woman of Samaria?' (For Jews have no dealings with Samaritans)" (John 4:7-9). She was expressing the common sentiment of the day--the Jews had no dealings with the Samaritans.

After Christ ascended, the church, including the apostles, continued to struggle with the issue of race. Peter had to be convinced by miracle to go and preach to a man who was not a Jew. Even after the miraculous vision recorded in Acts 10, he arrived at the man's house and said, "You yourselves know how unlawful it is for a Jew to associate with or to visit anyone of another nation, but God has shown me that I should not call any person common or unclean" (Acts 10:28-29).

Even after this Peter continued to struggle with dealing with those of other nations. He visited with Gentile Christians and ate with them, but when some Jews came he separated from his Gentile brothers for fear of the Jews. Barnabas was also caught up in Peter's actions, and he separated himself as well. Seeing the wrong in Peter's actions, Paul confronted him. Paul recounted the scene in these words:

> But when Cephas [Peter] came to Antioch, I opposed him to his face, because he stood condemned. For before certain men came from James, he was eating with the Gentiles, but when they came he drew back and separated himself, fearing the circumcision party. And the rest of the Jews acted hypocritically along with him, so that even Barnabas was led astray by their hypocrisy. But when I saw that their conduct was not in step with the Truth of the Gospel, I said to Cephas, before them all, "If you, though a Jew, live like a Gentile and not like a Jew, how can you force the Gentiles to live like Jews?" (Galatians 2:11-14)

The teaching of Jesus calls upon us to honor all men (1 Peter 2:17). The teaching of Jesus calls upon us pray for those that despitefully use us (Matthew 5:41-48). The teaching of Jesus calls upon us to esteem others better than ourselves (Philippians 2:3). The point I need you to understand is this. The coming of Jesus was not to cure social ills. Sadly, people will continue to mistreat one another. Our Lord came to die for the sins of the world. It is up to every person to learn His Word, to change his mind, and to follow His Teaching. This is how people and societies are changed. We must not continue waiting for God to do for us what He charged us to do for ourselves. When I change the world will get better.

Jesus Did Not Come to End Poverty

There were poor people before during and after our Lord's coming. If God desired to end poverty, He could have. The creator of heaven and earth could cure poverty, but that is not what we needed so it is not what God did. Near his death the Lord was sitting in a house owned by a man named Simeon. While he sat, a woman came in and anointed him with oil. The oil totaled about a year's worth of her earnings. The apostles were amazed to see that much cost poured out on the Lord. They called her actions a waste. Jesus said that she had anointed him for His burial (Mark 14:3-7).

Two things stand out about this interchange. First, the Lord was with them for a little while. Likely they did not realize how important the time they had with Him was or how short it was. Second, our Lord, in addressing the poor, said that there would always be poor people.

Christ teaches us to give to others. Galatians 6:10 teaches, "So then, as we have opportunity let us do good to everyone, and especially to those who are of the household of faith." This idea of a utopia on earth, though, does not come from the Lord. If God wanted Christ to do that, He could have. Nothing is too hard for the Lord? But there will be inequality as long as there are humans. God did not send Jesus to fix inequality. He left His Word so that we could. He did not send Jesus to die on the cross to remove poverty. You must not expect from God what God never promised to do. Stop praying about this and do what you can where you are with you have.

Let me share a quick life lesson with you: When I was young, I loved to play basketball. One day my brother Greg and I were playing in the park. At some point I noticed that this day was different than the others. We were playing one on one, and I could not score a basket. He was a little taller than I was at the time and was a lot stronger, so every time I tried to shoot he blocked my shot. This went on for a while. I moved to the left he moved also and blocked my shot. I went back and got the ball and made another move, and he blocked my shot. This went on for a while until I started traveling. I picked the ball up and ran away from him and tried to get a shot off, and he still blocked it. Finally, in frustration I screamed, "I quit," and started to walk off the court. He said, "You can't quit." I said, "Oh yes I can." I remember screaming at him, "Why do you hate me?" He said, "Boy, I don't hate you." I said, "You do, you keep blocking my shot. Every time I try to shoot you block it." By that point, tears were streaming down my face. I was excited, angry, and sad all at once.

At the time neither of us knew the magnitude of the moment, but he explained what he was doing to me. He said, "I want you to be better than I am. If you can learn to shoot over me and I am bigger, stronger and taller than you are. Then when you play people your own age you will have no problem with them. So you need to keep trying until you figure out a way to get a shot off." We were alone on the court that day, and that moment was amazing in shaping me as a person. I went back and tried and tried. He kept blocking some, but I did figure out a way to get up some shots. How does that help with understanding Christ's coming and poverty? I am glad you asked.

Since I know that Jesus came to die, I know there are a lot of things I cannot expect the Lord to do for me. When I talk to young people I hearken back to this moment. I tell young people not to confuse what Christ came to do with what they must do. In many high schools there are posters on the wall about how education affects earnings; these say high school graduates make more money than drop outs, so do not drop out. The posters also say that associate degreed people make more than high school graduates, this is followed by the fact that people with bachelor degrees make more than associates, and masters more than bachelor and it continues to go up from there. This poster is not about God. It is about how education affects potential earnings.

So I encourage young people to go to school and get an education. To accomplish this, they need to go to class on time, not loiter in the hallways or bathrooms. They need to sit in their classes facing the teachers, not turned sideways or backward facing their friends. They need to listen to the instruction being provided and ask questions if they do not understand that they are not to text and talk on their cell phones.

They need to study after school and sometimes before. They need to watch less television and read more books. They need to listen to their parents, and do what they say. They do not need to listen to their friends. They need to be polite and respectful to everyone. They need to live without drugs of all kinds including cigarettes, alcohol, and marijuana. They need to stop listening to people who tell them what they are not capable of doing.

I know it is hard and more difficult for some. I know there are disparities, but young people need to realize they do not have any choices. They can sit around making excuses, they can cry foul and even quit, or they can work hard and keep trying and figure out a way to get up a shot. No one is going to come along and give them a million dollars, including God. If they do not want to be poor, then they had better get to work.

If you think Jesus came to remove poverty, then I am sorry; you are in for grave disappointment. We will always have the poor with us. You just need to figure out if you are going to be a part of them. If you live in America, then you have a great chance to avoid poverty because, for all that is bad in the world, America remains one of the greatest places for one to amass wealth; that being said, remember where we began--are you sure you want to spend your life chasing after money?

Friend, you have been told the wrong thing. Religionists have taken God's spiritual work and confused it with the physical benefits of living in America. "We hold these truths to be self-evident, that all men are created equal, that they are endowed by their Creator with certain unalienable rights, that among these are life, liberty and the pursuit of happiness." These are the words of the Declaration of Independence. They provide the answer for the question the founders of this nation wanted to answer. This was the reason they were separating themselves from England. Some of the words are true. All men are created equal (Genesis 1:26-27), but, friend, the rest of this statement is not true. The way it is quoted, it appears we actually believe God said this. This is the work of the founders of the nation, it is not Scripture.

God never said that you had the right to life, liberty, and the pursuit of happiness. One of the things that God hates is hands that shed innocent blood. Every year in this country millions of babies never get life. If they had a right to it, why are they killed?

Does anyone have an objective and definitive answer for what pursuing happiness means? It is subjective and personal. So whatever that means to you the thought goes you have a God given right to pursue it.

I know this did not come from God because you might want to pursue something that is contrary to His Word. If you pursue something that God forbids, you should know you have no God-given authority to do such. What you will find is God condemning you and the act (1 Corinthians 6:9-11). You may not even have a constitutional right. What if something heinous is your pursuit of happiness? The law will stop you, arrest you, and force you not to pursue it.

To pursue any of these things is to live in opposition to God. By reading the above passages you might be tempted to fixate on the highly charged emotional issue of homosexuality. That serves to make my point. In America the founders envisioned citizens' being free to pursue their happiness. So politicians, activist special interests and many citizens are saying people have a right to pursue their own happiness. No one should say anything. If by "right" one means freedom to choose, then one does have that right, but if by "right" one means whatever one chooses is right, well, that is wrong. God is right, and in order for one to be right he must be in harmony with God's perfect character and God's revelation.

The problem is our founders made the statement that God has granted you this right, but God in not an American citizen and the Bible is not a declaration of independence for American citizens. What you can do as a citizen in America or anywhere else is not the same as what you can do in your relationship with God. If the words of our founders should be followed, then how much more should God's Word be followed and heeded.

There is no expression that says God gives every man the right to be free. If there were, how would one explain His own people's being put into bondage (Genesis 15:16)? Did Jesus have a right to be free? Then why was He born into bondage? There is an eternal amount of distance between what God says and what men say. Living in America is a great blessing, but living with God is not something our legislative, executive, or judiciary branches of government can dictate. The only right you have from God to pursue is to trust Him and obey Him, and the only source of information for your relationship with Him is the Bible. If God did not say it or promise, it then you should not expect it from Him.

Maybe we have been blind concerning the difference between life in America and life with God. Christianity is not a western or eastern religion, it is a heavenly religion. If we are in Christ, our citizenship is in heaven where Christ is (Colossians 3:1-5). Happiness is spiritual not physical. Jesus came to earth to die so that we could have spiritual life. Preaching today takes that notion and turns it into a carnal, physical grab-fest. This is the reason we are not happy. Christian friend, we need to open our eyes. "Open my eyes to what?" you might ask; that is the next thing we will discuss.

What Do You Think?

1. Why did Jesus come to earth?
2. What are some things Jesus accomplished on earth?
3. Why was a body prepared for the Lord?
4. What was God's Will for Jesus?
5. Why did Jesus not come to earth?
6. What rights does one have in his relationship with God?
7. How can God help with social problems?
8. How can one's expectations of God affect his relationship with God?

Chapter 7

Developing an Ability to See Spiritually

"Open Your Eyes so You can See"

Open Your Eyes so You Can See

The Bible uses the analogy of sight because of its power to move us to action. When we can see physically, life becomes abundantly easier. We can see where we are going. We can see what we are doing. We can see what we want and can go get it. The same thing is true of spiritual sight. When we can see God's spiritual Truths, our spiritual lives are made abundantly easier. In Christianity, spiritual sight is of greater importance than physical sight. Let me explain.

In John 9 we are introduced to a man who was born blind. The apostles believed that the man or his parents had done something wrong and that their sin was the reason for his blindness. This was the common thought of the day. Our Lord corrected their error and settled the matter forever. Neither the man nor his parents had done anything wrong. No physical disability is attributable to the sin of the person born with it, for children in the womb are not capable of doing either good or evil (Romans 9:11). In the context the Lord healed the man, then explained that the reason the man was born blind was to show God's glory (John 9:3).

There are many great lessons to glean from this chapter, but we only want to focus on one taken from the actual words of the man who was healed. While the Pharisees debated the legitimacy of the Lord's claim of being the Messiah, even calling Christ a sinner, the blind man focused on the results. He answered their false charges by saying, "Whether he is a sinner I do not know. One thing I do know, that though I was blind, now I see" (John 9:25). It is always hard to argue with Truth.

The open eyes of the blind man did three things. First, it validated the genuineness of Christ's claim. He truly is the son of God, the Savior of the world. Second, the open eyes of the blind man transformed his life. Suddenly he could see. The joy he felt had to be incredible. All the things he had imagined and thought could now be seen and realized. Sight is an amazing, wonderful blessing. He had lived in darkness, but now there was light. He had been led around, but now he could direct himself. He had been captive, but now he was free. Such is the incredible power of sight. His eyes were opened; he had been blind, but now he could see! Third, the open eyes of the blind man revealed who was really blind.

Jesus heard that they had cast him out, and having found him he said, do you believe in the Son of Man? He answered, And who is he, sir that I may believe in him? Jesus said, to him You have seen him, and it is he who is speaking to you. He said Lord, I believe, and he worshiped him (John 9:35-38).

The man had not simply been blind physically; he had not known the Christ; thus, he had been blind spiritually; suddenly, he was blind no more, he believed and worshipped the Lord. Conversely, the Pharisees were devout religiously, they could see physically, but they did not believe Jesus, so they would not worship Him; thus, they were blind spiritually. You see the real blind people in John 9, were the ones who could physically see all along.

The ability to see the spiritual realities God speaks about in His Word is far more important than seeing physically. People who are physically blind can obey God and go to heaven; people who are spiritually blind cannot. Physical blindness creates challenges in this life, but spiritual blindness will hurt you in this life and in the life to come. These reasons are why so many Bible writers wrote about spiritual blindness and warned against it. Sadly, it was God's own people who suffered from spiritual blindness (Isaiah 6:9-10).

Jeremiah spoke of it, "Hear this, O foolish and senseless people, who have eyes, but see not, who have ears but hear not" (Jeremiah

5:20). Ezekiel spoke of it, "Son of man, you dwell in the midst of a rebellious house, who have eyes to see, but see not, who have ears to hear, but hear not, for they are a rebellious house" (Ezekiel 12:2). The Lord echoed the sentiment of the prophets. His people had closed their minds to understanding God's Word. The result was this: Though they had the ability to see, they could not see. "Indeed, in their case the prophecy of Isaiah is fulfilled that says, You will indeed hear but never understand, and you will indeed see but never perceive" (Matthew 13:14).

The apostle Paul dealt with the same people who had refused to listen to Christ (Acts 13:40-41). They also rejected Paul's preaching. All of these warnings teach us one thing: You could be living a lie. You could believe a thing with all of your heart, and be wrong. You could believe it is true, you could think you see it clearly, and you could be totally in the dark. The prophets, the Lord, and the apostles are saying that you could have eyes to see, but you could be totally blind. But there is good news. The great thing about God is not simply that He is; it is not even that He made us in His image--do not get me wrong both are wonderful blessings--but maybe the greatest thing about God is that He communicated with us.

He told us that He is Spirit (John 4:24). He told us that His Word is Spirit (John 6:63). He told us that we need to see spiritually (Hebrews 11:1-3). He told us so we could open our eyes. The greatest thing about God is that He has communicated to man the things that are and the things that will be.

He told us so we would know how to live in this present world. He knows the spiritual realities exist whether we live by them or not. He also knows that when we violate His spiritual laws, we hurt ourselves. He told us, because what we do in this world will impact our lives in the next.

When we read the Bible, we are being given an opportunity to see this world for what it is and to open our eyes to see the unseen world we will live in eternally. If our eyes are open, we can see that which is unseen. If you never see spiritually, you can never be happy. The reason is that simple happiness can never be found in anything physical. Remember the three problems, nothing lasts, everything wears out, and we will die; therefore, we must look, we must see, beyond this world. We must see the things that are unseen.

Paul saw the spiritual. He suffered many things in his life. He was beaten, stoned, and left for dead. He had great anxiety for the care of Christians. He was shipwrecked and persecuted. He suffered hunger and was often in peril. He did all of this and he was single. Why does being single matter? Because he lacked the support, love, and encouragement a godly wife would have given him. And the thing that allowed Paul to live this life was that his eyes were open. He once was blind, but now he could see! We need spiritual eyesight (2 Corinthians 4:16-18).

God has told us three very important things, but to see them, we must open our eyes. We must see the world spiritually, and when we see them, they will change your lives. Once changed, we will certainly see that happiness is having our eyes opened. God told us.

The World is Temporal

Do you see this fact, or are you blind? God did not deceive us. He told us this world is temporary. When we see it, then it helps us appreciate that we have no need to try to live here forever. This world is passing away (Hebrews 1:10-12). That is not simply preacher talk. There is no new matter being created, and we are using the matter that is here, thereby making it more unusable. Since the world is passing away, we should not love it. And the world is passing away along with its desires, but whoever does the will of God abides forever (1 John 2:15-17).

Are your eyes open to this reality, or are you blind? This world is temporary. This is the reason God tells us not to lay up treasure here upon the earth:

> Do not lay up for yourselves treasures on earth, where moth and rust destroy and where thieves break in and steal, but lay up for yourselves treasures in heaven, where neither moth nor rust destroys and where thieves do not break in and steal. (Matthew 6:19-20)

The fleeting nature of money can be seen in how easy it is to lose. It could be here today and gone tomorrow. The rich farmer would have done well to learn this lesson (Luke 12:16-21). Nothing is said in the parable that suggests he did anything illegal to gain his money. Nothing is said that indicates that there was anything wrong with his being rich. Rather, the Lord took issue with how he lived for this world and did not plan for the next.

Our lives demonstrate whether or not we see this reality. This is not the kind of thing we can fake. If we believe this world is all there is, it is reasonable that we would live for this world. It makes sense to get as much as we can. It makes sense to horde all of our goods. It even makes sense to place more importance on possessions than people. The rich farmer did all of this, because he did not see the temporal nature of this world. On the other hand, if we see this world is temporal, then that will impact how we treat this world. Because faith must be lived, God constantly challenges our profession by asking for demonstration. "If then you have been raised with Christ, seek the things that are above, where Christ is seated at the right hand of God. Set your minds on things that are above, not on things that are on the earth" (Colossians 3:1-2).

If you see this, how are you living? Every, Christian must read these verses and answer the question. Where have I set my desires? Either they are fixed on things on the earth, or they are fixed on things in heaven. God is trying to tell us something, if we will only hear. God is trying to open our eyes, if only we will see.

Happiness is not under the sun, it is beyond the sun. This world is passing away. This is the reason Solomon could not find happiness under the sun. He only searched in physical things. Friend it is also why you will fail if you follow his search. Many religious people are blind to the fact that they are undertaking a search that has already been taken. If Solomon could have found happiness here in physical things, he would grabbed that happiness and exclaimed to the world, "Eureka, eureka! I have found it, I have found it!" He never did. He sadly stated, "'Vanity of vanity,' says the preacher, 'all is vanity'" (Ecclesiastes 1:2).

Unless you open your eyes and you stop looking on earth for something that can only be found in heaven, you will waste your life trying to catch the wind. You must open your eyes. This world is passing away; therefore, your eyes, desires, longings, money, and energy must be directed toward heaven and not earth. Do you have the eyes to see this? Take this quick test:

You might be blind if ...

- You put physical things above spiritual things.

- You love this world, and the things that are here, more than the next world and Who is there.
- You think things are more important than people.
- You place more emphasis on your physical man than you do on your spiritual man.
- You horde the things of this world believing the one with the most toys wins.

Let us not be like the Pharisees who thought they could see and were blind. Instead, let us be like the blind man, who was blind but could see.

Life is Short

Another thing that God told us is that our lives here are short. Do you have eyes to see this? Do you have ears to hear this? Do you have a heart to understand this? Or are you blind? Methuselah lived to be nine hundred an sixty-nine years old, and he died (Genesis 5:27). Nine hundred and sixty-nine years is an extremely long time, but it is nothing compared to eternity. He has been dead a lot longer than he was alive. No matter how long a person lives, this life is short compared to eternity. Do you have eyes to see this truth?

God desperately desires us to see this. Listen to how he described our time and our lives on earth. David said:

> But who am I, and what is my people, that we should be able thus to offer willingly? For all things come from you, and of your own have we given you. For we are strangers before you and sojourners, as all of our fathers were. Our days on earth are like a shadow, and there is no abiding. (1 Chronicles 29:14-15)

Did you catch that? Man's days are like a shadow, and there is no abiding. Our lives are not simply described as a shadow, but also like grass that withers away. The Psalmist contemplated his life in such terms, "My days are like an evening shadow; I wither away like grass" (Psalm 102:11). Life is also described as a vapor. James' instruction should serve as a sober warning to us all. "What is your life? For you are a mist [vapor] that appears for a little time and then vanishes" (James 4:14).

What a profound and alarming thought: Life is like a puff of smoke. Do you remember the steam from the tea kettle? When the water boiled, the steam went through the spout and the whistle sound was made. The next time you see and hear this, think about your life. The mist or vapor that escapes is your life. The vapor does not remain very long. This is what God is trying to tell us.

Life is described as the width of our hand, or a hand breadth. It is not a measurement we use today, so to understand it hold your hand in front of you with your palm up and squeeze your fingers together. The width of your hand is about three to four inches across. This is the length of your life. Again the Psalmist pled that he might understand how short his life was, "... my lifetime is as nothing before you. Surely all mankind stands as a mere breath" (Psalm 39:4-5).

Job also acknowledged the brevity of life, "Man who is born of woman is few days and full of trouble. He comes out like a flower and withers; he flees like a shadow and continues not" (Job 14:1-2).

We are not kept in the dark, or deceived, God would never do that. Instead, God told us repeatedly this world is temporal, so we ought not lay up treasure for ourselves here, and He told us that our lives here are short. Even the most aged person when compared to eternity did not live long at all. Dear friend, do you see this? There are no guarantees about life. Sadly, young and old some will end today.

Do you have eyes to see, or are you blind? Consider this.

You might be blind if ...

- You are focusing on the physical instead of the spiritual.
- You think you will be guaranteed to live a long life.
- You plan more for your future here than you do for your future in eternity.
- Your life after death does not determine your life before death.
- You are neglecting the things of today in anticipation of getting them together later.

Please, open your eyes; your life is a vapor, a shadow, a flower, a hand width; it is fleeting, and, friend, it is short! God also told us so that we could open our eyes and see. When we see this, we can live this.

Tomorrow is Not Promised

God told us this world is passing away, but for many that will seem too far away. God told us our life on earth is short. That gets closer to home, but many still convince themselves they will live to be old, so God went a step further in trying to open our eyes. God told us that tomorrow is not promised. Do you have eyes to see this or are you blind?

If you can see it, answer this question: "Have you lived your life as if you could have died yesterday?" or "Did you neglect, refuse, or fail to do something yesterday, because you would take care of it today?" What about this question: "Do you see that you could be dead by this time tomorrow?" Or maybe consider this: "Yesterday could have been the end of your life here, and the beginning of your life in eternity!"

Do you know the difference between December 6 and December 7, 1941? Do you know the difference between September 10 and 11, 2001? I am sure you know; look at the dates. The difference is simply one day. December 7, 1941 was the attack on America at Pearl Harbor. September 11, 2001 was the attack on America in New York. Friend, the sixth and the tenth respectfully were just one days difference from the seventh and eleventh; in each case, though, in one day thousands of people were ushered into eternity--whether they were ready or not. God tried to open men's eyes a long time ago, when He said, "Do not boast about tomorrow, for you do not know what a day may bring" (Proverbs 27:1). How powerful! We do not know what will be tomorrow.

Who knows what a day will bring? Our most precious commodity is now! Yesterday is gone, tomorrow is not promised; therefore, all we have for certain is now! This is the reason Scripture puts such an emphasis on what we do now.

Jesus said we should resolve church problems now. "So if you are offering your gift at the altar and there remember that your brother has something against you, leave your gift there before the altar and go. First be reconciled to your brother, and then come and offer your gift" (Matthew 5:23-24). Some folks should never make it through a worship service. Instead they should stop worshiping. They should leave the assembly and go to a quiet place in the building and solve their problems. Then they should come back and worship God acceptably. Instead, many come to worship God angry and hating their brothers. The Lord told us not to do this; I wonder do we have eyes to see it? You know, people have died while worshipping God. You are not promised tomorrow.

Paul said we should resolve relationship problems now. "Be angry and do not sin; do not let the sun go down on your anger" (Ephesians 4:26). You may have heard the joke. A husband and wife agreed not to go to bed angry. The husband said they had kept their commitment, but they had not slept in months. It may be funny, but how many are completely in the dark concerning God's Word and warning. Tomorrow is not promised; therefore, take care of the problems today. If you and your wife are angry at each other and are trying to have a relationship with God, please heed the warnings. Do not let the sun go down on your anger. Tomorrow is not promised. Peter warns that our refusal to treat each other as we should will hinder our prayers to God. "Likewise, husbands, live with your wives in an understanding way, showing honor to the woman as the weaker vessel, since they are heirs with you of the grace of life, so your prayers may not be hindered" (1 Peter 3:7).

The Holy Spirit says that we should resolve spiritual problems now. "Therefore, as the Holy Spirit says, Today, if you hear his voice do not harden your hearts as in the rebellion, on the day of testing in the wilderness" (Hebrews 3:7-8).

The saddest words ever uttered are "too late." How many people sit week after and week and hear the glorious Gospel of Jesus Christ, then leave the assembly without responding to God's invitation. Do they not believe? Have they not searched the Scripture to see if what is being preached is true (Acts 17:11)? Perhaps, do they believe they have more time? Are they blind to the Words of the Spirit?

"Today if you hear his voice do not harden your heart" (Hebrews 3:15). The reason is simply that tomorrow is not promised. What if this is your December 6? What if this is your September 10? This is not a scare tactic, and I do not mean to be insensitive. Read the passage above again. It is God's warning, it is God's plea, it is God's trying to get all to see that tomorrow is not promised. Do not boast about tomorrow, for you do not know what a day may bring (Proverbs 27:1).

This fact is an amazing and wonderful thing if you can see it, but is horrifyingly sad if you cannot. God wants our eyes open, so He gives us examples. He shows us people. He tells us parables. He teaches us lessons. He gives us warnings. Why? Because, friend, when you die, you are done affecting and impacting this world. Please think about that, your opportunity to change, help, and improve lives is now--it ends at the grave; your influence remains, but personally you can do no more good in this world.

When you die, you will never again give anyone good advice. You will never again tell another person here that you love them. You can never again say you are sorry. You can never right a wrong. You can never pay another complement. You can never see another smile. You will never again hold another baby, change another diaper, or hold another hand. The things you have said and done will be all that remain. The time you had with your children will be over. It will never again be what you wanted to say, it will always and only be what you said. Never again will you sing praise to God--on earth. You will never again study your Bible. You will never again help someone, hold someone, or share a special moment with another human being on earth. Do you see this? Are your eyes opened to it? Does your heart understand this fact?

You might be blind if ...

- You are still holding grudges--if you died yesterday holding a grudge, it would be held eternally.
- You are living unfaithfully to God--if you had died yesterday, that would be how you entered eternity.
- You think you know what will happen tomorrow.
- You think your biggest problem is physical.
- You spend today blaming someone else for your life.

Why Should This Make Us Happy?

Like the blind man who received his sight, we too were once blind, and, like him, our eyes have been opened by the Lord. Since we see, we can use the time we have properly. First, we should be concerned with finding God. Paul informed us that this is God's intent for all of us. God made the world and everything in it. He is not worshiped with man's hands because He does not need anything from man. He made of one blood all nations who dwell on the earth:

> That they should seek the LORD, if haply they might feel after him, and find him, though he be not far from everyone of us; For in him we live and move and have our being; as certain also

of your own poets have said, For we are also his offspring. (Acts 17:27-28)

Open eyes allow us to see that we will live on earth for a little while, but we will live in eternity forever. Therefore everyone's time here should be spent seeking the Lord and finding Him. Only a spiritually blind person would believe there are things more important than this.

Did you know that the reason you are here is to seek the Lord and find Him? The way to do that is to learn His Word and follow His Teaching. God's Word "is a lamp unto our feet and a light unto our path" (Psalm 119:105). It will guide and direct us to God. God's Word gives us understanding (Psalm 119:104). God's Word teaches us that Jesus Christ is "the way, the truth, and the life" (John 14:6). If your eyes are open, you should be seeking the Lord. If you have sought the Lord and found him through obedience to the Gospel (Mark 16:15-16, Acts 2:38; Acts 18:8; 1 Corinthians 15:1-4), then you should be happy that you have found the Lord, for nothing on earth is more important than finding the Lord!

Second, after you find the Lord, you need to make your family your priority. After finding God and obeying the Gospel of Jesus Christ, saving your family is the next most important thing to do with your life. Given the gravity and far reaching implications of our families, it is shameful that marriage is not given far more serious contemplation. It is a running joke that more time is spent on the wedding ceremonies than the marriages. There can be no doubt that this is due to people's having eyes to see, but not being able to see. The ceremony is for a few minutes or hours; marriage is for life.

Choosing a spouse should be the choice of a lifetime. Your eyes are closed if you spend more time contemplating furniture selection than spouse selection. You cannot see if you spend more thought on car financing than the character of the one you are about to marry. You are blind if you focus more on the physical than the spiritual when you choose a mate.

When you get married, you are choosing to give another human being total access to your life. Remember, you only have one life and remember that life is short. Giving someone else total access to it is a very serious thing--not only total access, but also total control. I know that does not sit well with many, but here is what I do not mean: I do not mean that you are no longer your own person; you are. Neither do I mean that you can no longer think for yourself; you can. Finally, I certainly do not mean that someone can hurt or harm you, but you can say or do nothing to stop it. Now, here is what I mean: When you are single, you have to answer to no one. When you are married, this changes. Your spouse reserves the right to ask and expect an answer for every aspect of your life. When you choose to leave the house, your spouse can ask, "Where are you going?", and you should tell him or her. When you choose to buy something, your spouse can ask, "How much did you spend?", and you should tell him or her.

When you say, "I want to have children," your spouse must have a say in this most important decision. When you say, "I want to live in this house or that neighborhood," or if you say that you want to work in this city, your spouse has a say in whether or not you will. If you are unwilling to give someone this kind of access and control over your life, then do not get married. You do not have enough time on earth to spend it violating God's Word in a marriage in which you do not intend to participate fully. No person can or should have such control and such access to your life as your spouse. If people contemplated these kinds of things before they got married, they would be much more selective in choosing a spouse. After finding God, loving our wives or respecting our husbands and bringing up our children in the Lord are the most important things any of us can do with our lives.

You can be happy if your eyes are open to see how important your marriage and family are. Your ears are not heavy, so you heard God when He said that your marriage mirrors His relationship with His people (Ephesians 5). Husbands, having a heart to understand, you know that your wife is as important to you, as the church is to Christ. You know that in your family, you stand in the place of God. You are a father to your children as God is to His people, and you are a husband to your wife as God is to His people. You know the joy you give them and the joy you receive from them. You know that your actions will impact your families not only for life on earth, but also for their eternal lives later.

Blindness is the only explanation for a man in this position putting his career before his family. Blindness is the only reason a man would speak harsh, critical words to his beautiful bride. Blindness is the only reason a father would not hug his son or have a tea party with his daughter. Blindness is the only reason a father would think his children will turn out right, even when he does wrong. Blindness is the only reason a father would believe buying presents is better than his presence. Blindness is the only reason a father would allow anything to have him separated from his wife or children. Blindness is the only reason a person could believe he could be a good Christian, yet be a bad husband and father. Blindness would be the only reason a husband would not allow his children to see him, laugh with his wife, share with his wife, hold his wife, and show affection to his wife. Blindness is the only explanation for one who thinks his children will believe, even if they do not see his belief (Ephesians 5:23-33; 1 Peter 3:7).

Blindness is the only explanation for a wife's not respecting her husband. Blindness is the only reason she would listen to mama and daddy more than she did her husband. Blindness is the only reason she would talk down to her husband. Blindness is the only reason she would disrespect her husband in front of her children. Blindness is the only reason she would try to rule over him and dictate to her husband. Blindness is the only explanation for her believing this would not negatively impact her children. Blindness is the only reason she could believe that this would be acceptable to God (Ephesians 5:22-24, 33; 1 Peter 3:1-6).

There have been many movies and books depicting the idea that a reality exists that people cannot see. All, in one way or another tell a story of a world within a world, but usually those living in the first world have no idea that the second exists. The Bible teaches the same basic concept. Unlike the movies, the Bible is true. In the movies the people are deceived; they believe their world is real, while being totally in the dark concerning the other world.

God did not do this to us. He did not create a world, and never tell us about the next world. The greatest gift from God is that He communicated with man. He did not deceive us or leave us in the dark. He told us our world is temporal. He told us we will only live here a little while, and, maybe most importantly, He told us our time here could end today. He told us so we could open our eyes.

He told us so we could seek the Lord and find Him. He told us so we could order our lives accordingly. He told us so we could live happy, holy lives now, and look forward to living with Him eternally. He told us; the only question is can we see it, or are we blind? It is always sad to hear of people dying, but sadder still is hearing people's reactions toward God. People begin to deny, denounce, and denigrate God. They are so sad that someone died "too soon." Or they ask where God was. Friend, loss is sad, but God did not cause the loss. He actually told us tomorrow is not promised. He told us, but how many people have read His Word and then ordered their lives accordingly? Happiness is not avoiding all hurt or harm, for we cannot. Happiness is having our eyes opened to life and its realization that the world is passing away. Life is short. Tomorrow is not promised.

If our eyes are opened, let us live today as if it were our last. Let us all love God today, as if it were our last. Let us all cherish our spouses, love our children, make wrongs right with our neighbors, and live faithfully for God today, for once we were blind, but, because of God's amazing love, now we see!

It is the love of God that makes all things possible. Take a fresh look at God's amazing love with me.

Remember, happiness is spiritual, and so is God's love.

What Do You Think?

1. What are some passages that use sight as a powerful teaching tool for God's people?
2. Who had sinned that the man in John 9 was born blind?
3. What three things were accomplished by the Lord's opening the blind man's eyes?
4. What is the greatest blessing that God has given man?
5. Who was really blind in John 9? Why?
6. What three things did God tell us about life?
7. What are some areas in life in which one may be blind?
8. If one's eyes are opened to what God says, what will be of concern to him?

Chapter 8

Appreciating the Reality of God's Love

"God Loves You Because God is Love"

There is nothing so important as love; we all need to love and be loved. We all need to know that God loves us. We need to belong. We need to feel a part. Above all, we need to see God's love--not in physical things, but rather in spiritual Truths. How many people have been given great gifts from their parents, but never knew love from their parents? How many people have everything they want, except for the love of the spouse who is providing the things? You could have everything you wanted physically, yet that would never indicate God's love for you; you see, the atheist next door has all the same things as you and he does not even believe in God. As God's child, you can know God's love, you can see God's love, you can understand, and you can be secure in God's love by reading and meditating upon His Word.

Maybe no other writer in the Bible spent as much time talking about God's love as the apostle John. He wrote about it so much that he is often referred to as "the apostle of love." He wrote five books in the New Testament, and all of them speak often about love. John penned what is arguably the best known passage in the entire Bible: "For God so loved the world, that he gave his only begotten Son, that whosoever believes in him should not perish but have everlasting life" (John 3:16).

While this may be among the most famous, it is hardly the only one in which John records Jesus' talking about love. "A new commandment I give to you, that you love one another: just as I have loved you, you also are to love one another. By this all people will know that you are my disciples, if you have love for one another" (John 13:34-35).

John also spent considerable time discussing God's love. Throughout his books, the point of loving one another is central; accordingly, it is shown that the love we are to have one for another is based upon the love God has for us. "Beloved, let us love one another for love is from God, and whoever loves has been born of God and knows God. Anyone who does not love does not know God, because God is love" (1 John 4:8).

Understanding God's love is essential to our happiness. The love of God must be the foundation on which we build our spiritual houses. I am and I belong because God loves me. God's love for us is the most comforting thought in the world, His love solidifies our place in the world, and it gives us strength to persevere through adversity. Additionally, it enables us to emulate his love in our lives. Loving and being loved is among the greatest keys to happiness in the world. Let us learn some things about God's love.

God's Love is Unconditional

In order to have a relationship with God, you must get to know the One with Whom you hope to have that relationship. Let me ask you a very important question: When I say God's love is unconditional, how do you understand the word "unconditional"?

Some think that because God loves me unconditionally, that means there are no conditions in our relationship. This is not what "God's love is unconditional" means. Others think that what we do determines God's love for us. This is not what "God's love is unconditional" means either. Both of these ideas are wrong, but many people hold one or the other of these views about God and His love.

The Biblical concept of unconditional love needs to be explained. When I say that God's love for you is unconditional, I am making a statement about God, not you. This is a statement about how God loves, or who God is. It is more easily understood when our focus is on God. May I suggest that you focus on God in every aspect of your relationship with Him?

To understand God's love, we must consider God's eternal nature. In Creation, man was created on day six. God existed before day six, because God is eternal; therefore, God loved man before He created man, because God was love before there even was a man to love. This is what John writes in 1 John 4:8: "If one does not know love he does not know God. For God is love." Stop and think about the phrase "God is love."

Here is the unconditional nature of God's love. This says nothing about how you behave. This says nothing about any conditions God would later put on your behavior. This is only a statement about God. In order to have a relationship with God, you must know Him. And, what you must know about Him is His eternal character. Everything He is, He is eternally. He is eternally holy, just, merciful, gracious, and loving. He is love, which means He has always been love; this also means that God cannot be or do anything else. He cannot change His eternal character. Our concept of love must be determined by God's character. His character is revealed to us in Scripture. The reason to study your Bible is to learn the character of God.

Please consider this as you interpret your life. You might be tempted to believe that when you do well, then God loves you, but when you do bad things, God does not love you, and He will not love you until you start to do good again. This conception of God's love hurts our relationship with God. It puts us in the position of constantly trying to get God to love us.

It is a very frustrating way of living, and if it is never corrected, it will lead you to despair. You will begin to believe you cannot please Him and that He is unfair and difficult for demanding so much of you. This despair can eventually lead to your leaving God and turning against God. Many people who hate God today at one point in their lives had loved God.

Properly understood, however, God's love provides our greatest motivation for loving Him back. This is especially true when we learn three things. The first thing you need to know is that God Loved You Before.

Before you were created

"And God saw everything that he had made, and behold, it was very good. And there was evening and there was morning, the sixth day" (Genesis 1:31). Remember God is eternal. He is from everlasting to everlasting; therefore, before He brought the world into existence, He was already love. It might even be argued that love in some part prompted God to create the world.

Before you were formed

God planned to use Jeremiah as a prophet before Jeremiah was born. He told Jeremiah that He knew him before he was formed, "Before I formed you in the womb I knew you, and before you were born I consecrated you; I appointed you a prophet to the nations" (Jeremiah 1:5). We all need to focus less on ourselves and more on God. He loves us before He forms us.

Before you did anything

Romans 9 is a great chapter about the sovereignty of God. To show God's sovereignty, Paul makes the case that God made choices to use certain people in His plan. Those people Paul would point out did not do anything to cause God to choose them; God chose. Among the examples are Jacob and Esau. Pay close attention to what Paul says about God's choice and the children's actions:

> And not only so, but also when Rebekah had conceived children, by one man, our forefather Isaac, though they were not yet born and had done nothing either good or bad-in order that God's purpose of election might continue, not because of works but because of him who calls-she was told the older will serve the younger. (Romans 9:10-12)

Here are three significant passages that all teach us one very important thing about God's love: God loved us before. He loved us before He created us, He loved us before we were formed in the womb, and He loved us before we could do anything good or bad.

The conclusion is inescapable: You cannot do anything to get God to love you, because He loved you before you could do anything! Love, like most things in life, is learned. You should learn to love at home. If no one teaches you, it will be difficult for you to love. The great thing is that even if we do not know how to love, we can learn how to love.

God will teach us; no doubt this is why God relates to us as our heavenly Father. As our Father, God loved us first so we could learn how to love. This is why the ideal way of parenting our children is to emulate the way our heavenly Father parents us. Considering that, answer this question for me: When did you start loving your child? Was it when he learned to walk, talk, read, write, or when he was potty trained? Or, did you love him when you first learned you were pregnant? If you began to love your child the moment you knew you were pregnant, then you loved him before.

Like God, you loved him before he was born. Like God, you loved him before he could see. You loved him before he could speak. You loved him before he could do anything. He did not have to earn your love. He was not so good that his goodness made you love him. No, before he could do or knew anything, you already loved him.

While writing this book, I visited a sister in the hospital. Days earlier she had delivered a baby. I sat and observed her and her husband's delight with their new son. Their joy was obvious, though she was still in some pain. I asked her when she started loving her son. Maybe wondering if it were a trick question, she paused and thought a moment. Then with conviction and certainty she said, "The moment I found out I was pregnant." I am sure you did as well.

We are capable of such love because God is our Father. Think about how much God loved you before. He loved you before you were created. He loved you before you did anything good or bad. He has never demanded you to act a certain way to get him to love you. He loved you before you could. This is what is meant by "God's love is unconditional."

You placed no conditions on your love for your child, because your child had your love before he could meet any conditions. What happens with our children happens with us as God's children. Our love for our children does not increase as they grow. Neither does God's love increase for His children. What happens is our children's appreciation for our love increases as they grow. Our appreciation of love--given before we even knew what love was--increases as we get older.

When you get older you learn how much your parents did for you before you could do anything for yourself; then, when you become a parent, you appreciate how tough a task parenting really is. Almost everyone who reaches this point calls or visits his parents to say, "Thank you," because now he knows that he never had to earn their love--he had been loved before he could. It also humbles us, because we realize we were totally dependent on someone else, yet they still chose to love us.

Think about that with God. God loved you before He formed you. His love for you has not grown over the years, but, hopefully, your appreciation for His love has grown as you have gotten older spiritually. It is also the reason for humility. We can be happy when we know that God loves us unconditionally. It was never my hair, height, size, shape, money, color, gender, smile, or anything physical--it has never been about me, it has always been about God.

Have you returned to your heavenly Father and said, "Thank you"? Maybe now would be a good time. Dear God thank you for loving us unconditionally.

God's Love is Universal

There is another aspect of God's love which we must learn and embrace. God's love is universal. We often put others down to build ourselves up. It is a lamentable part of human history. We fight and hate one another. We want for ourselves and not for others. For this reason, the idea of universal love seems like a fantasy; indeed, it would be if we were talking about man's love, but we are not; we are talking about God's love. If you will have a relationship with God, you must take a larger view of the world. It is tempting to view the world through all of our own small circles, but God is larger than my block and neighborhood. He is larger than my city and state. He is larger than my country and hemisphere.

He is the Ruler of heaven and earth. He is the Alpha and Omega. He is the Beginning and the End. He is the Almighty God. He has all power, and everything and everyone is subject to him. He is the Creator, Ruler, and God of all that is, but as large and powerful as God is, He has room to love you. You must find a way to understand that God loves you, personally.

You are part of the universe of God's universal love. It saddens me to know that people have no problem believing God is love, but they cannot also believe that God is love for them. Unfortunately, some people grow up in homes and environments where love is not shown. This has a profound impact on how they relate to God.

Our upbringing shapes our view not simply of people, but also of God. If our fathers were distant and cold, we are prone to think God is distant and cold. If our fathers were harsh and critical, we tend to think God is harsh and critical. If our fathers were perfectionists and were never pleased, then we struggle to believe that we can please God. If our fathers abandoned us, we believe God will abandon us as well.

This explains so much of our interaction with God. Our minds are like tape recorders, when we hear certain words and phrases the tape plays our preprogrammed songs (even if, or maybe especially if, we are hearing those words in a sermon).

When we hear that God is our Father, our mind plays the song labeled "father." When we hear our heavenly Father loves us, the songs for "father" and "love" are played. If those songs are painful and difficult, then understanding God's love reasonably becomes very difficult.

This must be understood if one will understand the second important fact about God's love. The second point is that God's love is universal. Remember God's love is unconditional. He loved you before you were created. You did not do anything to get Him to love you because He loved you before you could do anything. Now add to that this thought: God's love is universal. He loves you, or as I like to say, God loved you because.

Because He created the whole world

"For God so loved the world, that he gave his only begotten Son, that whosoever believes in him should not perish but have everlasting life" (John 3:16).

Remember that when God saw everything that He had made He concluded that it was very good. The creation included and was topped off by the creation of humanity. You are a part of God's wonderful creation. He made it; therefore, He loved it. You were part of that which God pronounced very good and no one is or can be excluded.

Because all men share His image

Paul preached the universality of God's love to unbelieving philosophers. They were just as included as any devout Jew and Paul himself. "And he made from one man every nation of mankind to live on all the face of the earth, having determined allotted periods and the boundaries of their dwelling place" (Acts 17:26). No one is excluded, because God's love is universal. All men are made in God's image; therefore, God loves all men.

Because all men are worthy of His love

The Lord's assessment of the world He created and the humans He created to inhabit it are summed up in this awesome passage: "For what will it profit a man if he gains the whole world and forfeits his soul? Or what shall a man give in return for his soul?" (Matthew 16:26). The Lord's death on the cross demonstrates God's love for man. The Lord's statement about the world demonstrates the worth of one human soul. If any of us could possess everything created, but lost his soul, his gain would not equal his loss. God's love is universal because every human being is worth His entire creation.

You are the height of God's physical creation. He loves you because you are a human being! Stop and think about that. There is no other reason needed for God to love you. After God created man He looked at His creation and said it was very good. God only created two people. Loving universally is not hard when the universe is two people, but God knew two would grow to several billion. He knew one day you would be one of them. He loves all men because He made all men.

Human beings are unique beings in the world. He made one blood of all men. There are only so many blood types. Thankfully, it does not matter what we look like anyone can use anyone else's blood if it matches. God crowned all men with glory and honor. Please appreciate the emphasis upon all men.

He created all men in His image. There are no humans who are sub-human. Whatever it is that makes us human, we all have it equally. In God's eyes, no one is unworthy; therefore, no one goes unloved by God, because he created everyone.

It is so sad that so many of us think so little of ourselves. A low estimate of oneself will cause one to have a low estimate of others. The reason is simple: Other people are just like you. Whatever you do not like about yourself, you will find that in other people. As a wise man once told me, "Folks are folks."

Our low thoughts of ourselves do not reflect God's thoughts of us. Please do not project your thoughts of yourself onto God. He thinks we are great. He thinks we are wonderful. He thinks what

He made is special and important. He loves us because of who we are. He knows the number of hairs on every one of our heads. He knows our favorite colors, desserts, songs, and shoes. He loves us for no other reason than that He made us.

No sparrow falls to the ground without God's knowledge. No lion goes hungry without God's knowing it. No flower dies without God's being aware of it. Now, consider that His care for none of them even comes close to the care and intimate knowledge God has of us. He shared His image with us. To not love us then on some level would be to not love Himself.

Your life will change immeasurably when you learn your worth. It is because we do not know it that explains why we spend so much of our short time on earth doing the things we do. Why do we spend so much time on physical things? Why do we spend so much time on clothes, shoes, hair, makeup, cars (all of which must be name brand)? Could it be that by these things we will convince ourselves and others that we are worthy of their love? Sadly, no matter how much we invest and spend, we never really feel good enough about ourselves or the ones we are trying to please. This would change if we knew that God's love was universal and it included every one of us equally. We know better, but we do not live better. We do not live in our lives what we try to teach our children; namely, that love is not earned, it is freely given.

Consider this: Like God, you started loving your children before they were born. And like God, you also loved them because they were born. What did they do at the hospital? Did they do something special? Did they sing a beautiful song? Did they deliver themselves? What did they do that was so great that by it you said, "Now I love them"?

Like all who have come before them. They did nothing. Except one vital and crucial thing: They were born. They did not need to do anything else, and, as we have already discussed, they could not. We waited for them to be born. We all went to the hospital hoping and waiting for them to come out. We were so anxious to see these persons whom we already loved.

Once we left the hospital, we brought them home. Likely, everything was ready. Their rooms were waiting for them. Their beds were waiting for them. Their clothes, shoes, and toys were all waiting for them. They were loved before they arrived.

In order to show them how much you loved them, one thing needed to happen. They just needed to be born. Then you could share with them the love you already had for them. Friend, the same is true for us. God created the world with us in mind. He formed it for us. Isaiah 45:12-18 tell us that God formed the earth to be inhabited.

Reading Genesis 1 is like watching parents prepare for the arrival of their children. God called for a light so He could work. He then separated the light from the darkness. He prepared the sky and expanse above the earth. He gave us food, the trees came forth bearing fruits and vegetables from the ground. He knew we would need seasons to grow those crops and to lighten our days and nights, so He commanded the sun, moon, and stars to shine for his children. He gave us fish and birds to eat, for one day, He knew, we would use them for this purpose. He did the same with animals on the land. He knew we would want them for pets, and need them for food.

Lovingly prepared, everything was ready. The sun was in the air. The grass was here. The sky was blue. The fish birds, animals, everything was ready, but something was missing. God spent five days preparing our room for us. He decorated it; He prepared it. The materials were here for our clothes, shelter, and food. God had prepared everything for us to show us how much He loved us; He just needed us to be born.

Then He did not speak us into existence. No, tenderly, gently he reached down into the clay and formed us with His own hands. Like a father's first kiss, God breathed life into us and we were made alive. He loved us before we were formed, and He loved us because He formed us. As good as those two things are, they are yet incomplete. Our understanding of God's love is complete when we understand a third point.

God's Love is Unlimited

This part of God's love maybe the most difficult for us to comprehend, because we often think in terms of cause and effect as it relates to love. We struggle with the notion that there is never a time when God does not love us. When people treat us well, we love them, but when we are mistreated, it affects and often hinders our love for them. This is not true of God. Remember, God is love. He loved us before He made us; therefore, there is nothing that we can do to impact God's love for us. God loved us because He made us; therefore, there is nothing we can do to get God to love us. God even loved us when we were in sin; therefore, there is nothing we can do to cause God to stop loving us. Sin is a terrible thing; it hurts and destroys all who partake of it. Since God's love was never based on our goodness, our sin does not stop Him from loving us. Listen to that again. Sin does not stop God from loving us. That did not say that sin does not hurt or could not even sever our relationship with God (Galatians 5:4). God's love is Who God is; our sin creates a problem for us with God. These things are not the same. The Bible teaches God loved us before, God loved us because, and God loved us when.

When we were in sin

> "For while we were still weak, at the right time Christ died for the ungodly. For one will scarcely die for a righteous person-though perhaps for a good person one would dare even to die-but God shows his love for us in that while we were sinners, Christ died for us" (Romans 5:6-8).

When we were at our worst, God sent His best. Christ died while we were sinners. This passage absolutely validates the first two points. God's love is Who God is. Since He loved us before we were created, He loved us before we did anything good or bad. Since He loved us because we were created, He loved for that reason and not for something we did. It is for these reasons that when we sinned and rebelled against God He still loved us.

Does sin hurt God? Yes, it does (Genesis 6:5-6). Can sin cause us to be separated from God, and that eternally? Yes, it can. However, Romans 5:6-8 is not about God's justice, it is about God's love; these verses say that God loved us while we were sinners. This means that God's love is not limited in anyway by our actions. He loves us even when we rebel against Him. Putting a few passages on love together please allow this paraphrase: "God so loved the world that he gave his only begotten Son, while we were sinners, to redeem us back to Himself." God loves sinners.

When we entered the kingdom

Very often we read Romans 5:6-8 to extol God's love, but we stop at verse 8. But Paul says some more things that are as important as telling us that God loved us while were sinners. He also tells us that God loves us when we become saved.

> Since, therefore, we have now been justified by his blood, much more shall we be saved by him from the wrath of God. For if while we were enemies we were reconciled to God by the death of his Son, much more, now that we are reconciled, shall we be saved by his life. More than that, we also rejoice in God through our Lord Jesus Christ, through whom we have now received reconciliation (Romans 5:9-11).

How sad it is that many of us understand God's love for us when we were in sin, but then we doubt that same love after we have obeyed God and are out of sin. Why is it more appealing and comforting to be loved as a sinner than as a saint? Paul is writing to the saints in Rome (Romans 1:7). They have obeyed the Gospel (Romans 6:3-4,16-17). They were once lost, but now they stand saved. God sent Christ while they were in sin.

This is why they were justified freely by his grace through the redemption that is in Christ Jesus (Romans 3:23-25). Because Christ came while they were sinners, it is imperative that they understand God's desire to save them now that they are saints. Hence the great encouraging words that follow (Romans 5:6-8).

Because we are justified, we will be saved from wrath. Remember, we were reconciled when we were enemies. Being reconciled we will be saved by His life. Because all of this is true, Paul says we also rejoice in God through our Lord Jesus Christ. We do not joy in ourselves. We do not joy in our good deeds. We do not joy in our great ability. No, we rejoice in God, through Jesus because He loved us when we were in sin, and he reconciled us when we were His enemies. We have nothing of which to boast; instead, we should humble ourselves and thank God for His amazing love.

When we stumble and fall

I trust that you are noting the progress: God loved us when--when we are sinners, when we obey the Gospel, when we enter the kingdom, and when within our faithful Christian walk, we stumble and fall. "But if we walk in the light, as he is in the light, we have fellowship with one another, and the blood of Jesus his Son cleanses us from all sin" (1 John 1:7). The unlimited nature of God's love can be seen in this passage. The walk of the faithful is a walk that includes provisions for sin. Remember, God loved before we could do anything good or bad; therefore, it was not our goodness that prompted God to love us.

Remember, God loved us when we were sinners. We were ungodly toward God. We treated him with less regard and honor than He is due, and He still loved us. He loved us when we became His children, but turned our backs on Him by walking in sin. Now justified, we walk in the light, and God continues to love us.

John writes of walking in the light. The walk is the manner of life. It is the mode of life that characterizes the child of God. That walk is in fellowship with God. That walk is conducted in the light, not in darkness. That walk is characterized by those who hate darkness and love the light, but that walk is one in which Christians may sin (1 John 2:1). What happens if a child of God, walking in the light, sins? Does God stop loving him? Please remember that it was not the child's walk that prompted God to love him in the first place. The verse says that the blood of Jesus keeps on cleansing us from all sin. A child of God may sin, but that sin is cleansed by the perpetual powerful cleansing blood of Jesus Christ.

In order to be happy, everyone needs to understand God's love. Scripturally, He never loves us more than He did before He created us. He loved us because we were born. He loved us while we were in sin. He even loves us when we stumble. The point is that God loves us before, during, and after conversion.

We must not focus on ourselves. Rather, we must try our best to understand God. What does, "God is love" mean to you? It is a statement of God's infinite character. God is eternal. Before He ever created a thing He was love. God never stops loving us. Please do not try to abuse or manipulate God's love. He knows our hearts; He cannot be mocked (1 Samuel 16:7; Galatians 6:7-8).

Do not try to take advantage of God. God is love, but this chapter has nothing to do with whatever God requires of men; rather, it has to do with the character of God. It is to provide the proper motivation for you to serve, love, and live for God. If you will be happy, you must understand God's love for you. Focus on God and not yourself.

There is something else you need to understand: God's love does not mean God will protect you from all harm. God will protect your spiritual life. No one can take you from God. No one can make God stop loving you. Your soul is protected. Remember, happiness is spiritual, but we live in a world within a world, and life on earth is filled with all kinds of challenges, problems, heartaches, and pain. If we suffer some of these, it does not mean God has stopped loving us. Read the next chapter and let me explain.

What Do You Think?

1. List some passages that speak about God's love.
2. Where does one's focus need to be in his relationship with God?
3. How does one's view of his father affect his view of God?
4. What is the ideal way to parent one's children?
5. What does "God's love in unconditional" mean? What does it not mean?
6. God loved man before, because, and when; what does this mean?
7. Are people more comfortable being loved as sinners or as saints?
8. How does one's knowing God loves him make him happy?

Chapter 9

Realizing the Universality of Time and Chance

"Time and Chance Happen to Us All"

Nothing calls God's love into question so much as the inadequacies of life. Children and adults lament the inconsistent bounce of life's ball. "Why did my loved one get cancer? He did everything right, he lived a good life, he loved God, he prayed, but he still got cancer." "Where was God when the gas leak killed my child, father, mother or wife?" "Why did I lose my job, house, family?" "Why did this happen or that happen to me, to us, to my child?" "Why did God not do something? I thought He loved me."

Man has been crying foul almost since God made him. Adam blamed God for giving him the woman who gave him the fruit, and Eve blamed the serpent for deceiving her. It is not fair is the cry heard around the world. Likely, everyone feels this way at some point in their life. It is not surprising. We feel this way because, to us, it is certainly true. Life is not fair, maybe that is true--we will discuss it. Whether you think it is or not, the good news is that we are not kept in the dark concerning life. God told us and recorded specific events for us so that we could realize that life can be harsh, cruel and painful. God knew that if we knew it, we would not be so discouraged when life was unfair to us, and that if we knew it, we would never question His love for us.

The Choices of Others

There are many ways in which life manifests its unfairness. One way is in the choices of others. Every human being is free. Every human being can make his own choices. This in part is the blessing of being made in the image of God (Genesis 1:26-27). What we learn from example and experience is that people sometimes chose to hurt other people. It is not fair. It is not right. It is, however, revealed and explained by God.

We can learn it as early as Genesis 4. Two men went to offer sacrifice to God. God accepted one man's sacrifice because he did it by faith; God rejected the other man and his offering because he did not offer it by faith. The man who was rejected became angry. What did he do? He chose to get the other man alone and kill him. Was this fair? Did the man who was accepted deserve this? Did God cause any of this? The answer to all of these questions is "No." You know these two men. One was named Cain, the other was named Abel. They were brothers. Cain murdered his brother because his own works were evil. "For this is the message that ye heard from the beginning, that we should love one another. Not as Cain, who was of that wicked one, and slew his brother. And wherefore slew he him? Because his own works were evil, and his brother's righteous" (1 John 3:11-12).

God made man free; therefore, Cain was free to choose his own actions. This is also the reason he was held responsible for what he did. Additionally, this is also the reason we are all held responsible for our actions (Genesis 4:9-15). We choose what we do, and so does everyone else.

We could multiply examples of people who suffered because someone else chose to hurt them. Who can ever forget what David did to Uriah (2 Samuel 11)? David slept with Uriah's wife, and to cover it up David had Uriah killed; God saw it all, and the thing David did displeased the LORD. Ahab wanted Naboth's vineyard. Ahab's wife Jezebel had Naboth killed so she could satisfy the petty desire of her husband (1 Kings 21). Judas agreed to betray Jesus for thirty pieces of silver (Matthew 26-27). What did the Lord do to deserve this? Joseph's ordeal was because of the choices of his brothers (Genesis 37:4-5). Daniel spent the night in a lion's den because of the jealousy of others (Daniel 6).

The reason these things happened then, is the same reason they happen now: You cannot have freedom of choice if God stops you from exercising it, but if He does not stop you from exercising it, you might choose to hurt someone--such is the nature of freedom. Everyone has it, even those who will sometime use it to hurt injure or even kill others. This is why there is a judgment. Fairness will be meted out by God. The Judge of all the earth will one day balance life's ledger. The warning from God is clear: Everyone will answer for what he does. "For we must all appear before the judgment seat of Christ, so that each one may receive what is due for what he has done in the body; whether good or evil" (2 Corinthians 5:10).

It is not the case that God has stopped loving us if someone chooses to hurt us; rather, they are making a decision for which they will one day answer to God. God's love is not based on our choices and it is certainly not based on the choices of others toward us. God is love.

Time and Chance

Another thing that demonstrates what is perceived as the unfairness of life is the combination of time and chance. Solomon said this happens to us all. It was one of the things he found out about life when he was searching for happiness. "I returned, and saw under the sun, that the race is not to the swift, nor the battle to the strong, neither yet bread to the wise, nor yet riches to men of understanding, nor yet favor to men of skill; but time and chance happens to them all" (Ecclesiastes 9:11).

What a helpful way of looking at life. Time and chance--you have probably seen these affecting your life. Question: Does the fastest man in the race always win? No, because sometimes things happen. Sometimes he gets a great start, but he pulls a hamstring. Sometimes he stumbles out of the blocks and never catches up. Is it fair? He trained for more than four years to run a race in under ten seconds, then he gets injured and loses? Is it fair that someone trained all that time only to false start twice and be disqualified? We might say "No," but these things happen. The fastest runner does not always win.

The battle is not always given to the strong. Sometimes the underdog wins, and that is, of course, why we play the games. In every sporting endeavor there have been upsets and surprises. From boxing, to college basketball, football, even Olympic hockey, the strongest team or person does not always win. The battle does not always go to the strong. Time and chance happen to us all.

Instead of using the expression "time and chance," we use the expressions "wrong place, wrong time" or "a fluke." When we use these terms, we are not describing some preconceived, planned act by God. We are acknowledging what God revealed to Solomon: Time and chance happen to us all. Think about that as it relates to tragedy, and it will help you to better deal with it. It is not a personal, unexplained plan of God. It is the time and chance elements of life.

Some who went to work on September 11, 2001, normally would have been off that day. Why did they happen to go in on that day? Maybe to get ahead on a special project, or maybe to fill-in for someone else, or maybe to make-up half a day before vacation. Whatever their reasons, likely some were at the World Trade Center that day who normally would have been off.

Like the rest of us, they had no idea what would happen that fateful day. They went to work and then planes were crashed into the buildings. Another person was supposed to be at work, and he called in and did not go. Still others missed one of the planes that was hijacked or made the plane. What we all need to know is that God had nothing to do with this event. God does not like one person more than another. Scripture goes out of its way to tell us that God is not a respecter of persons. "So Peter opened his mouth and said: Truly I understand that God shows no partiality, but in every nation anyone who fears him and does what is right is acceptable to him" (Acts 10:34-35).

God did not call one of them home. This is the absolute wrong concept of the event, of that day, and of God. Think about it. What changed about that day? What was different that day? Making the choice to go to work that day was not the problem. People barely make and miss flights every day. If the hijackers had not stolen the planes or flown them into the buildings, no one would have died. The reason the towers fell is because planes were crashed into them. Let us never forget that. Go back to the first point. Freedom of choice allows all men to choose.

Some men chose to steal planes and fly them into buildings, thereby taking the lives of many people. That choice coupled with the time and chance of life caused some to live and others to die. This is the explanation of the tragedies that have taken lives through the centuries. We can see the same thing with Pearl Harbor. We can see the same with both WWI and WWII. We can even see the same thing on the evening news. What if the young baby that was hit by the stray bullet had not gone outside? What if the person sitting in his living room when someone lost control and drove into his house had stopped in the kitchen?

The point is this: Time and chance happen to us all. Sometimes there is no rhyme, sometimes there is no reason. We live in a real world with real people making real choices. The choices that we or other people make have concrete consequences. "What if?" is a question we could spend our lives asking, yet never come up with an acceptable answer.

It is far better to realize that all men can choose, and that time and chance happen to us all. Is any of it fair? No. The point is not fairness as we perceive it; the point is we know it can happen. Knowing will help us avoid blaming God. Knowing also will help us to avoid thinking that God is picking on us. He did not take your loved one, despite what the well-intentioned, but misinformed preacher told you. He is not testing you. He is not punishing you. People can choose, and time and chance happen to us all. God is the only One telling you. The question is; are you listening to God?

Natural Disaster

Another way life's unfairness is manifest is in natural disasters, but, friend, natural disasters have been happening all over the world for a very long time. A famine drove Abram into Egypt (Genesis 12:10). There was a great earth quake in the days of the kings (Amos 1:1). The young man who left home was plagued by a famine. "And when he had spent all, there arose a mighty famine in that land; and he began to be in want" (Luke 15:14).

Natural disasters continue to happen today. A tornado can touch down and sweep through one community leaving it leveled to the ground. One block away not a single leaf falls to the ground. No car is damaged and no one is hurt. Who can explain why one block was destroyed, but another was not? Time and chance happen to us all.

Storms rage until they expire. Tornados run their course until they lose strength. Hurricanes, earthquakes, and volcanoes stop when they are done doing the damage they inflict. We do not stop them; neither is God wielding them on a string. They are not fair. Some people live, and some people die. Some property is destroyed, and some is untouched. These things do not have minds. We call them disasters because that is what they cause.

Thankfully, we have become very sophisticated in our ability to predict and track dangerous weather. The result is that we have gotten much better at giving advanced warning. The fact that we can predict dangerous weather is attributable to God, because the world God created is governed by law. The elements that make up our atmosphere are constant and consistent. This is why we can predict storms. Early detection allows us to warn those in harm's way much sooner than we once could. Because of technology many more lives are saved, but still natural disasters happen, and when they do, there is nothing fair about it.

These disasters are part of life on earth. Many believe they stem from the world-wide flood of Noah. Whether one believes that or not, it cannot be argued that storms and natural disasters are a part of our history. Earthquakes have been happening all over the world. They have destroyed both ancient and modern cities. These things are not fair, but they are the common lot of all men all over the world. It is not punishment from God, it is the reality of the world in which we live. Anyone saying he knows that God caused a natural disaster at best is wrong and misinformed, and is at worst lying. We need to remember that. We should take two things from natural disasters. One, we are not as powerful as we think. Two, we should be thankful God is. In His ministry, Jesus rebuked the winds and sea.

He said, Come. So Peter got out of the boat and walked on the water, and came to Jesus. But when he saw the wind, he was afraid, and beginning to sink, he cried out, Lord, save me. Jesus immediately reached out his hand, and took hold of him, saying to him, O you of little faith, why did you doubt? And when they got into the ship, the wind ceased (Matthew 14:29-32).

We should not spend our time begging mindless nature to be fair; rather, we should spend our time thanking Almighty God that He is. Time and chance explain the unexplainable path of natural disaster. Sometimes the choices we make can also impact the damage that is suffered.

Our Own Choices

Another thing that leads to troubles in life is not really something that is unfair, though many call it unfair. What many call unfair is nothing more than the consequences of their own choices. As noted, God made the world and the world is governed by law. One of the laws of God is the law of sowing and reaping (Galatians 6:7). We may not recognize it, but this law is what allows us to eat. We plant corn seeds; we reap corn. We plant orange seeds, and--because we reap oranges--one day we drink orange juice.

God established this law and order at the beginning (Genesis 1:11-12). This is why organic evolution has never been true and never will be. Every human came from a human, and this we know for certain. Every seed produces after its own kind. Stop believing the theories of man, and start believing God's Word which corresponds exactly with everything we know (not with the things men only theorize). Life comes from life--and that, of the same kind.

Many people are not aware that this law applies to human life as well. The law is simple: When you do things, those actions have consequences attached to them. You throw a rock into a still body of water, and you make a splash. Call the splash the act. What happens next is ripples form after the splash. The ripples are the results of the splash.

This is the way it is with our actions. We engage in an act; that act is the splash. Consequences follow the act; they are the ripples. You can no more reject, or deny, the consequences of your actions than you can the ripples from the splash. The rock was "sown" or thrown into the water; the ripples were "reaped" or naturally result from the throw.

God told us this so that we could sow spiritual things and reap spiritual things. He cautioned us against sowing to the flesh, because sowing to the flesh will produce destruction for our souls (Galatians 5:19-23). One chapter later Paul talks about the law of sowing and reaping, and he uses the same language. He talks about sowing to the flesh or sowing to the Spirit. Notice how the law works: "Do not be deceived: God is not mocked, for whatever one sows that will he also reap. For the one who sows to his own flesh, will from the flesh reap corruption, but the one who sows to the Spirit will from the Spirit reap eternal life" (Galatians 6:7-8).

The warning that starts the discussion should be sobering: "Do not be deceived." This law cannot be altered, and it cannot fail. What one sows is what he will reap. There are no mistakes; there is nothing unfair about it. It is as certain in life as it is in farming. It also has eternal implications. What is being discussed is not karma on earth; it is eternal salvation after life here is done. The one who sows to the Spirit, following the Spirit's Teaching, will certainly reap eternal life; conversely, the one who sows to the flesh will reap destruction.

Because this is unknown by many, they think life is unfair to them, and they think God is unfair when He does not intervene and stop their actions' consequences. As one preacher said, "People sow to the flesh, and then hope for crop failure." Consider that as it relates to sex. The law is this: If a man is capable and a woman is able, then when they have sex, she could become pregnant. This is not a miracle; it is the way God designed men and women. The sperm swims to the egg, and if one penetrates, conception is the result. This is the law of sowing and reaping. Everything living had seed put within it so that it could produce after its own kind--this includes humans (Genesis 1:26-28).

If one engages in sex and then becomes pregnant, is life suddenly unfair? There is no reason to cry foul and hate God and the world because you now have a child growing within you. If the young man who did this was not ready to be a father, he should not have done the thing necessary to become one. If the young woman who is now pregnant was not ready to be a mother, she should not have had sex. Having sex is how you get pregnant. The unfairness of life is not the problem here. God knows how He designed the human body and the world, so He says we should get married and then have children (1 Corinthians 7:1-5).

Neither is life unfair if the outcome of having sex is an "STD," a sexually transmitted disease. If having sex leads to your contracting a disease, please do not cry about life's being unfair. We could note many other examples in which the reason we suffer and cry foul is that our having made poor choices and ultimately paying for those choices.

Our choices and actions have consequences, and these consequences are built in. Many a person will cry foul about the unfairness of life. Sometimes it does seem unfair. God told us it would be. God allows every man to make his own choices--so sometimes it is not that life is unfair, we are simply suffering the consequences of our own choices.

If a man lies about his credentials to get a job and gets it, is that fair? If later it is found out that he lied and is fired, has life become unfair? In the Bible a man lied to David. He told David that he killed King Saul, David's enemy. He thought by saying so, David would reward him. Instead:

> David said to him, How is it you were not afraid to put out your hand to destroy the LORD's anointed? Then David called one of the young men and said, Go, execute him. And he struck him down so that he died. And David said to him, Your blood be on your head, for your own mouth has testified against you, saying, I have killed the LORD's anointed. (2 Samuel 1:14-16)

Are we reaping something that our own mouth has said? Is our own mouth's testifying against us? The Lord cautioned us about our words. He said we should be careful not to say too much. He taught us that our yes should be yes and our no should be no, for if we talk too much evil or sin could result (Matthew 5:37).

If a man steals and gets away with it, is life fair? If he is later found out and sent to jail, has life become unfair? We should not hope or want people to get away with doing bad things. We should be thankful to God that there are consequences for our actions. We need consequences. They help to keep us from doing harm to ourselves and others. There are consequences for stealing, drug dealing, and murder; there are also consequences for lying, cheating, and showing up late for work too often. Can you imagine life, if there were no consequences for our actions?

Some people want to be free, but do not want the consequences that come with that freedom. Let me ask you a question, how would you like it if every time you were about to make a choice, God stopped you from making it? Maybe you really found someone you loved--picture it--you like her smile, walk, and the way she laughs. She is a good person. She loves you, makes you smile, and has a great sense of humor. You have a lot in common. She really "gets" you. She does not want to change you, nor you her. If you are a man, you asked and she said, "Yes." If you are a woman, he asked and you said, "Yes." You decided that this was the person with whom you would spend the rest of your life, but before you could get married, God stopped you. He just said, "No." It will not work. You are not right for each other; you cannot marry this person.

While there are many who might say they wish God had done that, that is said after they were already married. No one would have wanted God to do that when they were making the decision to get married. People who are getting married are certain about the person they are marrying at the time. They have done the research. They have dated the person. They have strong feelings for the person. They are certain that they have found their soul mate. How dare someone tell them they are wrong--even God. If God stopped us from making our own choices what do you think we would do? That is easy. We would cry foul. We would call Him unfair. We would say that He does not trust us. We would ask Him why had He made the world and us at all, if He were going to decide for us. We would tell Him not to control us. We would tell Him to butt out of our business. We would shake our fists in the air at God. We would tell him how capable and intelligent we are. We would demand our freedom from this bondage. We would say we want to be free. Amazingly, we would tell God to do exactly what He has done.

You are free, and so is every other human being on earth. With freedom comes the possibility of pain, heartbreak, divorce, sickness and everything else we experience. He allows everyone to make his own choices. Sometimes that means man suffers. The good thing is this: God told us it would be this way.

Do You Want What You Deserve?

Before leaving this thought, let me add one more thing. Throughout this chapter, I have been using the phrase "life is unfair," to describe many things in life. While we say "life is unfair," I am not sure it really is, for what do we mean by fair? Are we saying that we should always get out of life exactly what is just or what is due a particular set of circumstances as if we could add up some formula that says given certain factors the outcome should be x? If so, it would seem life would be nothing more than a math equation.

If we all did get exactly what we deserved in any given set of circumstances, no one would like it. Have you ever done something silly or even dumb? Maybe run with a knife or, worse, play with a gun. Did you ever play with fire, jump off of a roof, tease a vicious dog, or drag race a friend.

What if any one of these things had gone differently? Would you still be here? Would someone else with whom you played still be here? We probably did a lot more than almost put someone's eye out. If we escaped these or any other things without harming yourself or someone else, what should we conclude? Should we say life is fair? Maybe we see life like getting change after a purchase. If the cashier does not give us enough change, he cheated us. Life is not fair. If the cashier gives us too much change, his mistake we got extra money. Life is fair.

Life works both ways. Sometimes we suffer having done nothing to warrant it; other times in fun or ignorance we do the most incredibly dumb things and no one gets hurt. It is not some Divine plan. It is not karma. It is not a cosmic happening in the world. It is human beings making decisions--some good, some bad--with no pre-planned outcome; life is the result of those choices. Think about that the next time something goes wrong or right.

Life is neither fair nor unfair, it is just life, and life has been happening to mankind since God made him. In Genesis 4 Cain killed Abel, and God held Cain accountable for his actions; however, He did not stop him, neither did He put a force field around Abel. He made man with choice, and it would be unloving not to allow him to exercise it. Happiness is not avoiding all of life's difficulties; it is having one's life built upon a solid foundation. Jesus Christ is the only rock that will stand through the storms of life (Matthew 7:24-28).

There is one more aspect of life that must be mentioned: God is working in the world; however, without revelation no one can accurately pinpoint God's exact acts. We know He is working because He told us to pray to Him, but it is not necessary that we know everything He is doing, because, whether we know it or not, He can still accomplish His Will, and it would defeat the purpose of trust if He told us everything He was doing. It is noteworthy that those in Scripture acknowledged their ignorance of God's specific actions when they were not told.

Paul met a runaway slave and taught him the Gospel. The man obeyed the Gospel and Paul wrote a letter to his master. The book of Philemon is the letter. In this letter Paul appealed to Philemon to receive Onesimus back, but he cautioned not merely to receive him back as a runaway slave, but also as a brother. Paul wanted Philemon to treat Onesimus as he would treat Paul if Paul came to visit. In this letter Paul broached the subject of why Onesimus ran away and how he came to meet him. Listen to what he says, "For this perhaps is why he was parted from you for a while, that you might have him back forever, no longer as a slave but more than a slave as a brother-especially to me, but how much more to you, both in the flesh and in the Lord" (Philemon 1:15-16).

Paul was careful not to say that God had caused Onesimus to run away so that they could meet and he could become a brother. He said perhaps this was the reason. We rejoice when anyone obeys the Lord, but we need not explain the events of life by claiming God did something that we have no knowledge of for sure. Life is not fair, God told us this. He also told us that He is watching over the world and His eyes and ears see us and are open to us; thankfully, God told us. This should be sufficient cause for us to be happy, especially since so much of life is the result of our own choices. Would we want anyone else making our decisions?

What Do You Think?

1. What are some ways life seems unfair?
2. How does life's unfairness affect one's thoughts about God's love?
3. Explain Galatians 6:7-8.
4. Is God working in the world?
5. How are consequences like throwing a rock in still water?
6. How do time and chance help to explain tragedy?
7. Would one desire God to stop him from making his own choices?
8. Discuss Philemon 1:15-16.

Chapter 10

A Picture of Redemption

"Jesus is God's Lamb, Not Ours"

Life can be difficult, and it does seem unfair. Women are far too frequently abused. Sadly, children are beaten, abused, and abandoned. People are murdered. Fortunes are stolen. A myriad of other things happen every day. All of which cause us to scratch our heads and wonder about life.

The simplest thing to do is to ask God to stop bad things from happening, but He cannot. The reason is much of life's pain, heartache, and trouble is caused by us, and, because God created us in his image, we have the ability to choose our actions. It is actually God's love for us that allows the pain and heartache we suffer, because love demands freedom; freedom necessities choice; and choice can lead to joy and pain. So instead of stopping us, changing us, or preventing us from choosing, God did the greatest thing He could for us: He redeemed us!

Sometimes as parents we say to our children, "You should be happy that ...," and then we will tell them something we have done for them--what we say is something that does not register to the children as something for which they should be happy. Usually, our children are sure that the thing they want is what would make them happy if only they could get it, but we know what is best for them, so that is what we give them. This is how it is with redemption. If we knew what God has done for us, redemption alone would be cause enough for us to be happy for a lifetime. Thankfully, God told us so we could know, and by knowing we can be happy about what He has already done for us.

Your Bible Has Only One "Story" in It

The Bible is the only book that tells us of our redemption. Unfortunately, many people see no point to the whole of the Bible. They have no understanding of Its unity. They simply believe it is a collection of stories that teach good moral principles. They are unaware that the Bible tells one amazing story; because of this misunderstanding, far too many people believe they cannot understand the Bible.

The result is frustration and disbelief. To many the Bible remains a closed book. They have access to It, but they do not believe they can understand It. It is so unfortunate, because they are robbed of the life changing power of God's Word. Their frustration flies in the face of why God gave His Word. Paul encouraged the Ephesians to read the letter he wrote them and they could understand what he wrote (Ephesians 3:4).

The Psalmist declared, "How sweet are your words to my taste, sweeter than honey to my mouth! Through your precepts I get understanding; therefore I hate every false way. Your word is a lamp to my feet and a light to my path" (Psalm 119:103-105).

God gave His Word so It could teach us about Him, and guide us to Him (Acts 17:24-26). It is written that we might believe that Jesus is the Son of God (John 20:30-31). In order to believe It, though, we must understand It. Dear friend, lasting happiness comes from understanding the Bible. The Bible tells only one Story. It has a beginning, a middle, and an end. It is like a great adventure, or maybe a great movie.

The Story's Conflict – Adam, Satan, and Sin

The adventure begins as soon as we open It. We are immediately captured with the words "In the beginning God created the heaven and the earth" (Genesis 1:1). Creation introduces us to the wonder, and power of our great God. We are told of our creation (Genesis 1:26-27; 2:7). Eternal questions are instantly answered. How did we get here? God made us. Where did men and women come from? Man came from the dirt, and woman came from man. How did the animals get their names? Adam named them, man was made intelligent.

Why are we social beings? We started in marriage. We started in a home. It is not good for man to be alone is God's Divine commentary on us as beings (Genesis 2:18). We are told all of these things in the beginning of the Bible. We are told of the beautiful garden of God where he placed man to live. In creation we were made perfect. Mankind was made pure, innocent, and he communed with God. All of this and more is the amazing wonder of Genesis 1 and 2.

By Genesis 3, we are introduced to a new character, Satan. We will learn much more about him later in the Bible, but in the garden he works through the serpent. He lied to Eve and she disobeyed God. She took of the forbidden fruit and gave it to her husband, who was with her, and he also ate. The beauty of perfection was now destroyed. The peace that had prevailed gave way to chaos and confusion.

The day mankind sinned was, arguably, the darkest day in human history. Their eyes were opened. They felt new, different, no doubt strange emotions, things they had never felt before. They felt shame and guilt so they covered themselves. They felt fear, so they hid themselves. This is all recorded in Genesis 3:6-7.

God came to visit Adam and Eve, no doubt as he often had, but this time they were hiding from God, so He called to them, and Adam answered. God asked Adam a series of questions. The questions were for Adam's benefit. God knows everything, so He knew the answers to these questions (Genesis 3:9-12).

He asked Adam of his location. "Where are you?" He asked of his Adam's new knowledge, "Who told you that you were naked?" He asked Adam of his obedience, "Have you eaten of the tree of which I forbade you to eat?"

After Adam's answers indicted Eve, God turned His attention to Eve. He also asked her a question: "What have you done?" This is a great question. We need the rest of the Bible, and maybe our lives, to fully appreciate it. In Genesis 3, it is impossible to know the full extent of the answer to that question. Eve's answers indicted the Devil, who used the serpent to deceive her (Genesis 3:13).

Still, in Genesis 3 God punished everyone involved. Adam, Eve and the Devil were all punished for their roles in this sin. If you have not read Genesis 3 in a while, may I suggest you do so? For it is the beginning of the unfolding of the story of the Bible. It is the place where God asks you to have a seat while He begins to tell you how He redeemed you.

God stopped working when he created the world (Genesis 2:1-2). Nothing was lacking; everything he made was very good (Genesis 1:30-31), but, now that man had sinned, things were not very good anymore. Because of sin, God had to go back to work; this time He was not creating a physical world as He already had. This work involved how to overcome sin. How would God redeem mankind back to Himself? This work is spiritual redemption. The story of the Bible is how God saves man, how God redeems mankind back to Himself. It is the greatest story ever told.

The Story's Climax Foreshadowed – Abraham and Isaac

Have you seen a Polaroid picture? They were great. You took the picture and then slowly, but surely, the picture came into view. It was fascinating to watch this unfold, and to wait to see exactly what was taken. We can do that with redemption. There is a picture taken, a Polaroid if you will, of how God redeemed humanity. The picture is taken in Genesis 22, let's look at the photo together and see how it comes together. It really is a beautiful picture.

Suppose you and your spouse wanted a child. You tried everything imaginable, but you could not have one; nevertheless, after many years of sadness, at last there was hope. You were told that something could be done. It turned out to be true, but it took another twenty-five years to happen. At last, after twenty-five years of waiting, you were going to have a baby.

I imagine the day of your baby's birth would be like no day you had ever experienced. You had thought about what it would be like, but nothing could have prepared you for the reality. Holding a new born baby is humbling beyond words. The thought of that young life's depending on you is staggering. It can literally knock you to your knees. It is one of the few times when men are not ashamed to cry or even faint. They might be counted worthy of praise if they do either, or both.

Each day would be a new adventure as your baby grew. You would take pleasure in his baby steps. You would walk and talk together. You would teach him about life. You would share stories. You would instill traditions. If you had one, you would pass on the family business. Your life would be great. Likely, you would thank God continually for your child.

But can you imagine if one day, out of the blue, God spoke to you and said something like this: "Take now your son, your only son, Isaac, who you love ... and offer him for a burnt offering ..."

That is right; you heard me. What if God told you to offer your one and only son for a burnt offering to Him? Would you? Could you kill your son and sacrifice him to God? We are never told why this was said to Abraham. There is no record that Abraham was given any further instruction than what we read in Genesis 22:2; yet this is precisely what he was told to do.

The request God makes is incredible, but the response and actions of Abraham are equally incredible. God said, "Offer your son to me," and Abraham woke up early in the morning to go do what God had said. If ever there were a day to sleep in, this would have been it; rather, Abraham woke up early. He took the proper equipment, the things necessary for a sacrifice. He took fire, wood, a knife, and Isaac. He woke up early and he woke up Isaac as well.

Abraham was committed; he had to be. The journey took three days. This tells us that he had time to think about what he was going to do. They travelled a day and had to pitch a tent for the night. They woke up and travelled again and had to pitch a tent for the night. He had time to think about what he was going to do. It is far easier to perform a courageous act for God in an instant than it is to be faithfully committed to God for a lifetime. Abraham was committed to God.

Abraham was convinced. He told his young men that he and Isaac would go away, worship, and return to them (Genesis 22:5). Amazingly, he knew he was going to kill his son, yet he included Isaac in the return trip. Another interesting thing about this journey is that up to this point Abraham is the only one who knows what he is going to do; that is, until Isaac speaks. Most estimate him to be a teenager at this time. What he asked would have understandably stopped almost any father in his tracks. They walked together to the place of sacrifice. "And Isaac said to his father Abraham, My father! And he said, Here am I my son. He said; Behold the fire and the wood: but where is the lamb for a burnt offering" (Genesis 22:7).

Can you picture it? He is the sacrifice, and he does not even know it. Talk about the innocence and trust of a child. Abraham's answer was full of power and faith in his heavenly Father. Without missing a beat (I doubt he even broke stride), Abraham said, "God will provide for himself the lamb for a burnt offering; my son, So they went both of them together" (Genesis 22:8).

Abraham did not wait around for God to provide a sacrifice. He continued to the spot. He laid the wood in order. Can you see the makeshift altar in your mind? He laid his son down on the wood and tied him to it. What must Isaac have been thinking at that moment?

Better yet, what do you think Abraham saw, in the eyes of his beloved son? He drew his knife back. Time must have stood still. Maybe he was sweating from the heat and stress of the moment. How hard was his heart pounding? How fast was Isaac's beating? Would his son die at his own hands?

Just here we need to pause, for we have taken the picture. The Polaroid film has begun to slide through the camera. In Genesis 22, God stopped Abraham's hand. An angel from heaven called his name twice. "Abraham, Abraham do not lay your hand upon the child" (Genesis 22:10-12). The sacrifice was stopped, and Abraham passed the test. Behind him a ram was caught in the bushes. Abraham removed his son from the altar. He retrieved the ram, and offered it instead of Isaac.

The New Testament books of Hebrews and James both speak about this event. Faith is the topic of discussion in both books. Both writers put the offering of Isaac in the past tense. The authors are keenly aware that Isaac was not killed by Abraham's hand, but they are viewing the event through Abraham's eyes and intention. The faith Abraham displayed is worthy of emulation.

In his heart he had killed Isaac, and he would have done it physically, had he not been stopped. Hebrews 11:17-19 gives us more insight into Abraham's mind:

> By faith Abraham, when he was tested, offered up Isaac: and he who had received the promises was in the act of offering up his only son, of whom it was said, Through Isaac shall your offspring be named. He considered that God was able even to raise him from the dead, from which, figuratively speaking, he did receive him back.

The record reads that Abraham offered Isaac. The King James Version says that he "offered his only begotten son." These are powerful statements. Interestingly, we are told Abraham's thoughts as he offered Isaac. Abraham believed that if he killed his son, then God would raise him from the dead.

This is what enabled him to offer him. Again, the King James Version of the Bible uses the word "resurrection" to describe Abraham receiving Isaac back from the dead. Stating that he was resurrected, and in a manner he was, because Abraham did kill him. Isaac was dead to Abraham who believed God would make him stand again. It is a great event. It is a great chapter, but this was not written to be an explanation of Genesis 22. There is much more here than meets the eye.

Remember, God created the world with you in mind (Isaiah 45:15-18). If life ever knocks you down, or things seem particularly hard, consider that God loved you before you were born. God loved you because you were born. Sadly, humanity sinned and ruined God's creation. "By one man sin entered the world and death by sin" (Romans 5:12). "For all have sinned and come short of God's glory" (Romans 3:23). "If we say we have no sin, we deceive ourselves and the truth is not in us" (1 John 1:8). Because of sin, God went back to work. What God did next may be even more amazing than creation.

Remember Isaac's question: "Father, I see the wood, and the fire, but where is the lamb?" Abraham's answer is the answer of all time: "Son, God will provide himself a lamb for a sacrifice." And, friend, he did. God provided Himself a Lamb. Look at the content of the chapter. There is a father and a son. Isaac is referred to as Abraham's son, his only son, whom he loves. The book of Hebrews calls Isaac Abraham's "only begotten son." There is an altar, and the father laid his son upon it. There is an instrument of death. Abraham had a knife in his hand. He drew that knife back and the father killed his only begotten son. And what was that Hebrews 11 revealed about Abraham's thoughts? He thought his son would be resurrected, if he were killed. The father sacrificed his son. What a story!

The Story's Climax – Jesus, the Lamb of God

Dear friend, this is the story of the Bible, and the story of human history. It is a perfect portrait of the matchless love of God. When we shake the Polaroid that was taken, we are amazed at what we see. The picture revealed on the Polaroid is not Abraham's offering Isaac; rather, the picture is God's sacrificing Christ. Our Heavenly Father provided Himself a Lamb, because He knew there was nothing we could provide for ourselves.

When Adam and Eve sinned, they were put out of the garden. Their sin cost them access to the tree of life. Death was their punishment and eternity awaited them. How could they get back? What could they do to make things right with God? What could they do to cleanse themselves from their sins? If you answered, "Nothing," then you are correct. Left to themselves, they had no answer for the problem of sin.

Humanity had and continues to have no answer for the problem of sin. Please do note the shift from what could Adam and Eve do to humanity had no answer. You see, all of humanity was in Adam and Eve. Their problem was everyone's problem. Your problem and my problem is ultimately a sin problem. No man, please think about that, no man at any time and in any place could do anything on his own to resolve it. Listen to this pertinent, penetrating question from Proverbs, and please tell me your answer to this question: "Who can say, I have made my heart pure; I am clean from my sin?" (Proverbs 20:9). The only answer is, no one.

If ever we needed anything from God, it was redemption. God needed to provide Himself a Lamb, because no one else could. Of course, God knew this and so He did. Abraham could not have been more accurate. Happiness is ours when we understand this. The entire Old Testament and the Gospel of the New Testament furnish us with God's provision. The prophets prophesied of one who was to come; Jesus is God's Lamb. "The next day he [John] saw Jesus coming toward him, and said, Behold the Lamb of God, who takes away the sin of the world" (John 1:29)!

The death of Christ is God's sacrificing His Son, His only begotten Son, Whom He loves. Please do not miss this point. "For God so loved the world that he gave his only begotten son," is about God! This is redemption. We did not appease God. He provided His own appeasement. We could do nothing. So God provided Himself a Lamb. The phrase "of God" shows ownership. Jesus is the lamb, of God or God's lamb. The church belongs to Christ thus it is the church of Christ, or Christ's church. The Scripture is revealed by the Spirit thus Paul says, "Take the sword of the Spirit, which is the word of God" (Ephesians 6:17). Christ is the Lamb of God, He is not our Lamb. Isaiah 53 paints a vivid and painful portrait of our Savior, God's Lamb. As you read it, think about this: Abraham's son was spared; God did not spare His own Son (Romans 8:32).

Jesus is God's Lamb, Not Ours

Isaiah opens chapter 53 by describing the Savior's birth and rearing. He is described as a man of sorrows and acquainted with grief. He is shunned and avoided. It sounds like the Lord led a lonely and painful life. If you think Abraham's love for Isaac was great, how much more did God love His Son? Isaiah turns his attention to us in the next section: "We hid our faces from him. We went astray. We all turned to our own way. And God laid on him the iniquity of us all."

Unlike us, he was oppressed and afflicted. Like a lamb, he was brought before men for slaughter. Along the way, he did not open his mouth. He was arrested falsely. He was taken and put into prison. All of this was done to Him because of our sins. He had none of His own and through it all He never did any violence; neither, did He say any wicked or evil thing.

Finally, Isaiah turns his attention to God. It pleased God to bruise Him. He put Him to grief. He made Himself an offering for sin. He is God's Lamb. He would fulfill God's pleasure. God would not turn away from His sacrifice. He laid Him on the altar. He drew the knife back.

Isaiah makes it clear: "He [God] shall see the travail of his soul, and he shall be satisfied." God's sacrifice would justify many. Christ pleased God, because He poured out Himself unto death. Jesus Christ did not become sin. He was God's Offering for sin. God provided Himself a Lamb! It is the greatest story ever told. It is the greatest act ever done. It is the greatest gift ever given.

The Bible is God's telling us how He did that for us. He called Abraham, Isaac, and Jacob. Jacob's sons produced the twelve tribes of Israel. Moses was called to deliver them from Egyptian bondage. Joshua took them into the Promised Land. Judges ruled them for hundreds of years. David was called to be king over God's nation. From David's family, Christ came. Jesus Christ is the Son of Abraham and the Son of David (Matthew 1:1).

He is the Seed promised to Abraham through Whom God would bless the world (Galatians 3:16). Jesus is the Seed of David, Who would build God's house and kingdom (Matthew 16:18-19, 1 Timothy 3:15-16). Jesus is God's Lamb, Who would be slain for the sins of the world. All of this time, all of this effort, all of this action on God's part was to bring His Lamb into the world. When Jesus came to earth, He made it clear. He was here to do His Father's Will and to finish His work:

> Meanwhile the disciples were urging him, saying Rabbi, eat. But he said to them, I have food to eat that you do not know about. So the disciples said to one another, Has anyone brought him something to eat? Jesus said to them, My food is to do the will of him who sent me and to accomplish his work. (John 4:31-34)

He said He came to die for the sins of the world. He came to give His life a ransom. He laid down His life for His sheep. We had nothing to do with God's Lamb's coming. God planned this in eternity. Man was not created until day six. Before there was a beginning in Genesis, God had already planned our redemption in Christ. Paul says the plan was purposed in eternity (Ephesians 3:9-11).

We snapped a picture in Genesis 22. As we shake the picture and wait, slowly the image begins to shine through. The longer we look, the more it comes into focus. When at last it is clear, we do not see a picture of Abraham and Isaac; rather, we see a picture God laying His Son upon a cross and sacrificing Him for you and me. Here is the answer to a happy, holy life. Here is the reason to live for God. Here is the liberty you seek. The whole issue rests in God. He gave, He saves, it is not about us, it is all about Him. The sooner we realize this the sooner we can know lasting happiness.

We receive his grace and demonstrate our faith in Him (Hebrews 11:6) by happily and humbly doing what He says, trusting what He has done. The Polaroid is God's laying Jesus, His only begotten Son, on a cross. He gave His Son for his enemies. He gave His Son for liars and thieves, for fornicators and adulterers, for hypocrites, for gossips, for envious sinners like you and me. If God's giving His only Son Whom He loved on a cross to die for us is not sufficient cause for us to be happy, then, friend, what is? This is why Psalm 32 says, "Blessed is the man whose sins are covered."

Redemption is Our Happiness

Redemption should put joy in our hearts, smile on our faces, and songs on our lips. Others, when they are seeing us, when they are hearing us, when they are worshipping with us should be able to tell that we are redeemed. If sin is understood, if God is understood, if Christ is understood, if redemption is understood, then those who are redeemed should be happy.

This is what is so horrific about physical carnal religion. It takes this great spiritual gift and cheapens it. It denigrates the glorious gift of Jesus by asking God for toys and trinkets. People are happier if they think God is giving them a few dollars than they are God giving the priceless gift of Jesus. How sad must heaven be when God sees this from those who profess belief in Him.

What if I asked you, and you answered honestly; what would you want most from God: a billion dollars or redemption in Jesus Christ? Consider a line formed before two curtains. Behind one curtain was redemption through Jesus Christ. Behind the other curtain was a billion dollars. A single file lined was formed and we were all in it. Each person could choose their curtain. Which one would you choose? If you say redemption then if you have it, why aren't you happy? If you would say a billion dollars than friend you will never truly be happy, and here is why?

You can buy things with your money, but things cannot give lasting happiness, you already got things. You could go places you're your billion dollars but places can only give temporary joy. You can have lots of friends, but people cannot give you lasting happiness. At some point no matter what you do you will run into the same problems Solomon did. Your billion dollars will cease to give pleasure, it will wear out, someone might steal it and no matter what you do with it, you will die; what will you do about death, billionaires also die. Billionaires get sick, their homes get destroyed in storms, their families have problems also.

However, if you are redeemed by Christ your sins will be forgiven, your conscience will be clear, you will live a happy life now and an eternal life with God in heaven. Do you believe these passages?

- Better is a little with the fear of the Lord than great treasure and trouble with it. Better is a dinner of herbs where love is than a fattened ox and hatred with it (Proverbs 15:16-17).

- Better is a little with righteousness than great revenues with injustice (Proverbs 16:8).
- Blessed is the one whose transgression is forgiven, whose sin is covered. Blessed is the man against whom the LORD counts no iniquity, and in whose spirit there is no deceit (Psalms 32:2-3).

God did for us what was best for us--He redeemed us. If you chose Him, and you are redeemed, then why are you not happy?

What Do You Think?

1. What attribute of God's Word enables it to guide man?
2. What is the story of the Bible?
3. What was God's request of Abraham?
4. What things indicate Abraham's willingness to obey God?
5. What is man's biggest problem?
6. James and Hebrews speak of Abraham's offering Isaac; what do they say?
7. How is Genesis 22 illustrative of God and Christ?
8. Why should one be happy if he is redeemed?

Chapter 11

A Picture of Man

"Every Human is Crowned with Glory and Honor"

But what if I am redeemed, but I am still not happy? What if I am struggling even though I know I am redeemed? First, check your mindset; are you focusing on the physical? A physical mindset will have trouble seeing spiritual Truths, especially as it relates to obedience and forgiveness. Second, check your belief. A physical mindset will also focus on human ability rather than God's character or teaching. If you are, then you are struggling with living faithfully and your issue may be your lack of belief. For many, being redeemed is more challenging than comforting because they feel as if they fail at Christianity more than they succeed. It might feel like calling customer service and trying to get help solving a problem; let me explain.

How often have you spoken to someone in customer service only to be terribly disappointed? I know, probably too many times to count. It is so bad that one talk show host refers to customer service as "customer no service." Banks may be the worst. If you have an overdraft, it shows up instantly and almost permanently; on the other hand, should they do something wrong, getting your money back is like pulling teeth. It is as if your money booked a suite at the roach motel--money checks in, but it does not check out, at least not easily.

This is not coming from a disgruntled bank customer; okay, maybe it is. The real point, though, is that the people you end up talking to are not empowered to solve your problem. They have the unenviable task of dealing with your problem while having no power to solve it. There is not much worse than being charged with a task, but not being equipped to accomplish it.

This situation is actually frustrating to both parties. The one who has the expectation is disappointed; he is not getting what he wants. He desires it, he has made the person aware of it, but it is still not being done. The one dealing with the customer's expectations is also disappointed. He is aware of the task, he is willing to do it, but he is certain that he cannot do it. Try as he might, he lacks the power to do what is expected; understandably, the expectations continue.

This must have been the situation between Rachel and Jacob concerning children. Jacob loved Rachel and did all he could to please her. The problem was that Leah, Rachel's sister, had many children, while Rachel had none, though she wanted them desperately. Seeing Leah's four sons, while having none of her own, had to be very difficult for Rachel.

Rachel's disappointment reached a head, and she confronted Jacob about it. Genesis 30:1 tells us, "When Rachel saw that she bore Jacob no children, she envied her sister. She said to Jacob, Give me children, or I shall die!" Jacob is the one who is expected to do something, but he is not empowered to do it. It is not the case that he could not father a child, for He had fathered four with Leah; rather, it was the case that God saw that Leah was hated and allowed her to bear children (Genesis 29:31-35); therefore, Jacob could do nothing to grant Rachel's request. He did not have the power to do it.

We are not told how often Rachel spoke to him about this; neither are we told of any past responses Jacob gave. The response that is recorded demonstrates Jacob's frustration. Genesis 30:2 records "Jacob's anger was kindled against Rachel, and he said, 'Am I in the place of God, who has withheld from you the fruit of the womb?'" He was angry. He was not in the place of God. No doubt he wanted to give her children. No doubt he had tried to give her children, but he could not; accordingly, he was angry that she was asking him to do that which he could not.

Do you know this feeling? Do you feel like you are being asked to do that which you cannot? I fear that many Christians feel this way. Not just at work, home, or play; but also that many Christians feel this way about their relationship with God. They are certain that God calls upon them to live a certain kind of life. They are also certain that God expects that they will have joy in Christ, but they feel just as strongly that they cannot do it. Like Jacob, they feel like they are expected to do something, but they think they have no power accomplish it; still the expectations continue. Like Jacob, when you feel this way long enough, you will become frustrated, angry, and maybe even give up.

Some may feel they are incapable of being what God wants because of their pasts. Maybe, like me, you have made a lot of mistakes. If you make enough mistakes, you start feeling like living for God is impossible. It is true that doing wrong can make it very difficult to believe that you are capable of doing better. "Someone can do it," you tell yourself, "but not me." Maybe you feel like it takes a special person, a superhero of faith, to be what God wants. Friend, I cannot impress upon you strongly enough how wrong this kind of thinking is.

The same thing is true when it comes to happiness. Some have convinced themselves that they will never be happy. They have God, they have Christ, but they do not have happiness. They have concluded that being happy is not for them. Instead, they have resigned themselves to misery. Thus resolved, they spend their time trying to figure out a way to live miserably but comfortably. It is kind of like trying to figure out a way to walk comfortably with a tack in your shoe.

Others feel the same way, but they cannot come to terms with the misery. Instead, they have opted to claim that the Holy Spirit does everything for them. They live more in fantasy than reality, but they call it faith. Really, it is little more than religious superstition. No matter what happens in their lives they attribute it to the actions of the Holy Spirit.

If they get a job, parking space, or extra change from the cashier, the Holy Spirit did it. If they get fired, get into an accident, or get sick, the Holy Spirit did it. If they win the lottery, find some money, or benefit even from wrong doing, it was all the blessing of the Holy Spirit.

Because life has beaten them down so badly, they feel completely powerless; therefore, they attribute everything to the Holy Spirit. This makes them free from responsibility, free from dealing with life, free from choosing or getting better, because the Holy Spirit does it for them. With this mindset, Christianity makes no sense, because good, bad, or indifferent, they did not have anything to do with their lives--the Holy Spirit does it all.

These are the two ways many people live their lives: One is resolved to misery and is trying to live with it; the other is miserable but denies it, choosing rather to let the Holy Spirit live for him. Neither is happy. Both claim to love God and to have a meaningful relationship with him. Neither actually enjoys any of the benefits of said relationship.

With all of my heart, I beg you not to allow this to be your life. Please do not give up on being happy and settle for misery, and please do not accept the rejection of God's Word and Its objective Truth in favor of subjective feelings, hunches, guesses, and senses to explain life. Let us go to Scripture, let us trust God, let us believe him, and let us appreciate that God calls upon us to choose Him, to love Him, to yield to Him and to be joyous in Him for only one reason: because we can. We can because God only expects of us what He has empowered us to do! Happiness is knowing God has empowered us.

I believe Psalm 8 records words spoken by an angel to God, revealed to man and recorded by inspiration. Not everyone agrees with this position. First, let me say it is not something about which I would be dogmatic. Second, ultimately it is not really important who said it; what is important is what is said about humanity. Third, let me set forth the reasons I believe it.

The passage is quoted in the book of Hebrews 2:6-8. The passages leading up to those passages are about angels. Hebrews 1:4 shows Christ is better than angels. Hebrews 1:5 shows God never called one of the angels His son. Hebrews 1:6 teaches that when God brought Christ into the world, all of the angels worshipped Christ. Hebrews 1:7 says angels are spirits who are God's ministers. Hebrews 1:8-12 are about Christ. Unlike angels, Christ is Divine--His throne is forever and ever.

Hebrews 1:13 and 14 return to the angels. No angel has ever been told to sit on God's right hand. That they (angels) are all ministering spirits is repeated. This time the additional thought is added they work on behalf of humanity. Chapter 2 continues the thoughts begun in chapter 1. The "therefore" connects the two chapters. The subject of verse 1 is the audience and writer. He says therefore they should give great attention or more heed to the things they had heard. What they had heard was the Gospel of Jesus Christ. It is admittedly compared to the law that Israel of old had heard.

Hebrews 2:2 says that the Word spoken to Israel was spoken by angels. According to the writer the Word spoken by angels to Moses was authoritative and everyone who transgressed it was judged accordingly. The writer then tells his audience that if they reject what they had heard spoken by Christ it is less likely that they would escape condemnation (Hebrews 2:3-4), because as he has already proven, Christ is superior to angels. Hebrews 2:5 makes the statement that God has not subjected the world to come to angels.

Hebrews 2:6 is the verse that is the subject of potential disagreement. It reads:

- "But one in a certain place testified, saying, What is man, that thou art mindful of him? or the son of man, that thou visitest him?" (KVJ)
- "But one hath somewhere testified, saying, What is man, that thou art mindful of him? Or the son of man, that thou visitest him?" (ASV)
- "It has been testified somewhere, What is man, that you are mindful of him, or the son of man, that you care for him?" (ESV)

Other renderings are basically the same. The question is who is the one who testifies or says, "What is man?" By starting in chapter 1:4, I have tried to show that the context is overwhelmingly about angels. They are compared to Christ. Christ is superior. Christ is Divine. Christ is worshipped by angels. Christ is God's Son, and Christ sits on His throne. Angels are ministering spirits.

Beyond chapter 2:6, the context immediately returns to angels. Note from Hebrews 2:7 that man is made a little lower than the angels, that man is crowned with glory and honor, and that man is set over the works of God's hand. Compare that last statement with what was said in verses 5 and 6:

> For unto angels hath he not put in subjection the world to come, where of we speak, But one in a certain place testified saying, What is man that thou art mindful of him? or the son of man that thou visitest him?

Listen to the question; verse 5 says the world was not put in subjection to angels, verse 7 says God has set man over the works of His hands, verse 6 asks the question, "What is man?" The question stems from who was put over the works of God's hands. In light of the fact that angels are heavenly beings, one might ask God how could you put a lesser being over the works of your hands and not an angel?

Additionally, Hebrews 2:8 continues the quote of Psalm 8 and Hebrews 2:9 shifts to Christ. Jesus Christ was made a man, thus Jesus who is superior to angels was made a little lower than angels that he might taste death for all men. Hebrews 2:10-15 continue the consideration of Christ and His work in our redemption. Hebrews 2:16 makes the point that Christ did not take on the nature of angels, rather He took on flesh and blood and became human.

I believe the overall context has three beings in the discussion: Christ, angels, and humanity. Hebrews 1:4, 5, 6, 7, 13, 14; 2:2, 5, 7, 9, and 16 have the word "angel" in the verses. The question seems to be what is man that God would put him over the works of his hands and not put angels in this position? What is man that God would crown him with glory and honor and make him a little lower than the angels? What is man that Christ who is superior to angels would lower Himself and become a man? The question seems to me to come from a heavenly view downward. It seems to come from a third party perspective. The one in a certain place said, "When I consider thy heavens, the work of thy fingers, the moon and the stars, which thou hast ordained, what is man?" It sounds like a first person inspection of heaven and earth with a question, after the inspection, directed to God.

I say all of that because I believe it, is said by an angel, but let me say again--what is important is what was said. This is what empowers us. What is said is spoken by someone who observed things about humanity. The things that were said are true; this is what makes them so powerful.

So, please eavesdrop with me on a conversation an angel had with God about us. The angel was not upset, but he was curious. He had no ill-will toward man; neither did he mean to insult men. He appeared perplexed about how much time and interest God invested in man. Imagine looking at earth and man from the angel's point of view. After praising God note his comparison:

> O LORD our Lord, how majestic is your name in all the earth! You have set your glory above the heavens. . . . When I look at your heavens, the work of your fingers, the moon and the stars, which you have set in place, what is man, that you are mindful of him, and the son of man, that you care for him? Yet you have made him a little lower than the heavenly beings, and crowned him with glory and honor. You have given him dominion over the works of your hands; you have put all things under his feet, all sheep and oxen, and also the beasts of the field; The birds of the heavens, and the fish of the sea, and whatsoever passes along the paths of the seas. O LORD our Lord, how majestic is thy name in all the earth! (Psalm 8)

There are four important things about man that we can learn from this Psalm. The angel states these things as true. He has observed them as things God has done for man, and he is questioning God about them. He has considered God's creation. Specifically, he looks at what must be among the grandest parts of God's creation the sun, moon, and stars. What an amazing view angels must have of these things.

They are in no danger of being burned up by the sun. They have an understanding of the multiplied million, maybe billions, of stars that exist. They have insight into the vast, vast distance of the creation. Light years are not years at all to angels. What an amazing view of God's masterful work. This angel looks at it all, then looks at man and comes to his question.

"When I look at your heavens, the moon and stars the works of your hands. What is man God that you are mindful of him? And what is man that you take care of him?" After his question come four things about man. Each statement the angel makes clearly demonstrates how God has empowered us.

The First is Our Worth

Our worth is captured in the phrase "made him a little lower than the angels." The angel says God did this. God made man a little lower than angels. Angels are great and powerful beings. They are God's ministers. They work on behalf of humanity. I do not think this angel is disgruntled. I think he is surprised.

From his vantage point, the sun, moon, and stars are very impressive. In comparison, man does not look like very much. He certainly does not look worthy of the level of interest God pays him. What is man? The answer is that mankind is made a little lower than the angels.

Unfortunately, most people do not think of themselves this way. Consider that the angel knows God, himself, and man. He recognizes that God made man a little lower than angels. This means human beings have intrinsic worth. We do not gain this worth by what we do. We have it because God made us. Everyone in heaven knows it; sadly, few people on earth do.

The comparison to the sun, moon, and stars is really no comparison at all. Human beings are the zenith of God's creative efforts. The sun, moon and stars are grand and magnificent. They light our days and illuminate our nights. They determine our seasons and immeasurably aid our lives, but they have no life within them. They do not think. They do not reason, consider, reflect, or decide. They do what they do because they are designed to do it. They are inanimate objects, not living beings. They are not made a little lower than angels; we are.

When our Lord wanted to help men understand the value of their souls, He also used the creation as an example. The Lord asked what it would profit a man if he gained the whole world but lost his soul, what would a man give in exchange for his soul (Matthew 16:26). It is noteworthy that the word "world" in the passage means the orderly, arranged universe. Our Lord is speaking about the same thing as the angel.

The entire creation is compared to man. This includes the sun, moon, stars, and everything else. The Lord's point is: If it were possible for a man to possess the entire universe, but he lost his soul; then the universe would not be enough to equal the loss. This is why the Lord asks, "What will a man give in exchange for his soul?" Our souls are worth more than a billion dollars, they are worth the whole world.

What an overwhelming point. Please think about it, consider it, and, more importantly, believe it. You could possess the whole universe, but if you lost your soul, the whole universe would not be enough to pay for it. This means that one human being's soul is worth more than all of the material creation. Let us go a little further.

Not simply is one human being's soul worth the whole universe, but every human being is worth the entire universe. Make it more personal. You, just you, only you, are worth the entire universe. You are worth more to God than the sun, moon, stars, and everything else He created. Please think about this, consider this, and believe it. It is high time that you pick your head up and start living like you believe God. The next time you pass a mirror think about that. Maybe you should say it to yourself as you look in the mirror. Wow! You are looking at someone who is worth more than the whole world.

It is true if you are poor, it is true if you male or female, it is true if you are struggling with sin. It is true if you are young or old, if you are blind or can see. It is true if you are healthy or terminal, it is true if a storm just destroyed your home, or if your spouse just said I want a divorce. It is true, God did it the angel observed it, inspiration recorded it. Your child is worth your house and everything in it, and God's children are worth the whole world He made for them.

How empowering is that? Whatever you think of angels, know that you are made a little lower than them. Before we leave this point, consider this: Jesus is the creator of both the universe and man. "All things were made by him, and without him nothing was made" (John 1:1-3). He would certainly know what part of His creation was most valuable and He said it was you.

The Second is Esteem

God's esteem for us is recognized by the angel. Esteem has to do with how highly God thinks of us. The thought is captured in the phrase "crowned him with glory and honor." God not only made man a little lower than angels, but the angel acknowledges that God has also crowned us with glory and honor.

Every human being is an amazing, splendid demonstration of the wisdom of God. Each person is crowned with glory and honor. David must have known this very well. Listen to him speak about God and man: "For you formed my inward parts; you knitted me together in my mother's womb. I praise you for I am fearfully and wonderfully made" (Psalm 139:13-14).

The angel says you have been crowned with glory and honor. The tenderness and care of David's words are enough to melt the heart. No parent could describe his love for his child better. How would you feel if I met you and said, "it is my pleasure to meet you? I think you are glorious and honorable?" No doubt, it would feel good, right? Here is the good part: Even if we never meet, and even if no one ever says it to you, it is still true: God crowned you with glory and honor.

You might not feel this way. Maybe your family or life has caused you to believe something different about yourself. Maybe your dad never told you so, or maybe he abandoned you. Maybe boyfriends did everything but make you feel this way about yourself. Maybe you and your friends called yourselves everything but honorable. I can understand why you might not feel this way, but what if I could prove it to you?

If I could prove that you are crowned with glory and honor, would you believe it? I submit to you that I have absolute proof that you are crowned with glory and honor. This proof is so concrete that to not believe it would be equivalent to denying your own existence. Before I set forth my proof, let me ask you one more time, "If I could prove it to you, would you believe it and start to live like it?"

Proof # 1: God shared Himself with man

Do you think God is crowned with glory and honor?

> Then God said, Let us make man in our image, after our likeness. And let them have dominion over the fish of the sea and over the birds of the heavens and over the livestock and over all the earth and over every creeping thing that creeps on the earth. So God created man in his own image, in the image of God he created him; male and female he created them. (Genesis 1:26-27)

If God is crowned with glory and honor, how can those who share His image be anything less? We are made in the image of God. This can be said of no other part of creation. Man is composed of body, soul, and spirit (1 Thessalonians 5:23). Our bodies will return to the dust (Genesis 3:19), but our souls will live eternally (Matthew 16:26). We are glorious eternal beings. God formed the spirit of man within him (Zechariah 12:1). He is the Father of spirits

(Hebrews 12:9). Our spirits return to Him when we die (Ecclesiastes 12:7). He crowned us with glory and honor when He made us in His image.

Imagine how different we would talk and treat others if we thought every human being was glorious and honorable. Think of the greatest celebrity you can imagine. How you would behave around him if you could get an audience with him. Your heart would race. Maybe your palms would sweat. You might even lose your breath. Why? The answer is simple. We think celebrities are glorious and worthy of honor. We have this so backward. We hold them up because of what they have done.

Instead, we should hold all men in honor because of who they are. All men are made in the image of God. All men are crowned with glory and honor. Start with yourself. Look in the mirror. Listen to what God thinks of His image. "Whoever sheds the blood of man by man shall his blood be shed, for God made man in his own image" (Genesis 9:6). God thinks His image is special and since you share it that makes you special.

Proof # 2: God became one of us

He did not simply share His image with us; He came to earth and shared our image.

- In the beginning was the Word, and the Word was with God, and the Word was God. He was in the beginning with God. All things were made through him, and without him was not anything made that was made. . . . And the Word became flesh and dwelt among us, and we have seen his glory, glory as of the only Son from the Father, full of grace and truth (John 1:1-3,14).
- "Behold, the virgin shall conceive and bear a son, and they shall call his name Immanuel (which means, God with us)" (Matthew 1:23).
- "But when the fullness of time had come, God sent forth his Son, born of woman, born under the law" (Galatians 4:4). John said the apostles saw, touched and handled God (1 John 1:1-2).
- Have this mind among yourselves, which is yours in Christ Jesus, who though he was in the form of God, did not count equality with God a thing to be grasped, but made himself

nothing, taking the form of a servant, being born in the likeness of men. And being found in human form, he humbled himself by becoming obedient to the point of death, even death on a cross (Philippians 2:5-8).

- "Philip said to him, Lord, show us the Father and it is enough for us. Jesus said to him, Have I been with you so long, and you still do not know me, Philip? Whoever has seen me has seen the Father. How can you say, Show us the Father" (John 14:8-9).

If you do not believe human beings are crowned with glory and honor, what do you believe about God? For God, the eternal One, came to earth and became human. If Christ is crowned with glory and honor, then every human being is crowned with glory and honor, for Christ was human.

Proof # 3: God died for man

Without doubt, the death of God the Son on Calvary testifies to the glory and honor of humanity. When God redeemed us, He bought us. This is why Scripture frequently speaks of our being purchased. The price of an item is indicative of what is the determined value of that item. This means that the amount paid is equal to the item, and vice versa. In other words, if one is willing to pay ten thousand dollars for a car, and if he had ten thousand dollars in cash, then he would accept that the car he is getting is equal to him in worth as the cash he is giving.

When it comes to purchasing man back from sin, what was the price? Listen to the Scriptures:

- Forasmuch as ye know that ye were not redeemed with corruptible things, as silver and gold from your vain conversation received by tradition from your fathers; But with the precious blood of Christ, as of a lamb without blemish and without spot. (1 Peter 2:18-19)
- For you are bought with a price, so glorify God in your body. (1 Corinthians 6:20)
- For I delivered to you as of first importance what I also received: that Christ died for our sins in accordance with the Scriptures. (1 Corinthians 15:3)

Christ paid His blood to redeem humanity. That can only mean that the worth of humanity is the blood of Christ. Whatever you think is the worth of the blood shed of Christ, is what you must think of humanity! Is the death of Christ glorious and honorable? How can that for which it was shed be less?

Hebrews 2 quotes the words of the angel recorded in Psalm 8. Verse 7 says man is crowned with glory and honor. Verse 9 speaks about Christ; note what it says: "But we see him who for a little while was made lower than angels, namely Jesus crowned with glory and honor because of the suffering of death, so that by the grace of God he might taste death for everyone."

I have proven it beyond a shadow of doubt. You are crowned with glory and honor. And the proof stands even if you refuse it, reject it, or discount it. But I pray you do not. Whatever God asks us to do, He is asking of beings he crowned with glory and honor. No one is unworthy, no one is incapable. We are esteemed by God because of who we are. We should be happy to view ourselves as God views us.

The Third is Trust

Back to the angel, next he describes how much God trusts man. The phrase is, "given him dominion over the works of your hands." To have dominion is to rule. When God created us, He said, "Let them have dominion" (Genesis 1:26). This seems somewhat curious to the angel. Remember the question, what is man? Here again is a good indication of just what God thinks of man.

The angel recognizes the reality that God put man, not angels, over the works of his hands (Hebrews 2:5). It should not be thought strange that this is the case. Man is just that special. Man is just that trustworthy. It is because man is unique among all of God's creation. To demonstrate this, please consider that there are four kinds of nature revealed in Scripture.

The first is the Divine nature; this is the nature of God. God is spirit (John 4:24). The word "God" does not describe a number, neither does it indicate a name. It describes a nature. It means Divine, or Deity. If one has this nature, then He is God, or Divine. Depending on the translation, one will read "godhead" or "divine nature" (Acts 17:29; Romans 1:20; Colossians 2:9). The Divine

Nature is eternal. God has no beginning or end. He is from everlasting to everlasting (Psalm 90:1-2).

The Divine nature is also all-powerful, all-knowing, and all-present. God is perfect in character, absolute in all of His ways. There are three beings that possess this Divine Nature: they are the Father, the Son, and the Holy Spirit. These Beings make up the Godhead. There is one Divine nature; it is possessed by three beings.

The second is Angelic nature; angels are spiritual beings; however, they are created beings. Since no angel is eternal, no angel can ever be called God. John tried to worship an angel and he was stopped. The angel told him that he was John's fellow servant, and that John must worship God (Revelation 19:10). Angels are ministers of God (Hebrews 1:7,14). They serve Him and do His Will. They are not humans; they are not Divine. They are greater in power and might than men (2 Peter 2:11). They fly. They appear in the shape of men. They disappear into fire (Judges 13:20). They are special, powerful, and created spiritual beings.

Next in descending order is humanity; however, let me say a word about animal nature then return to men. Animal nature is less than humanity. Of the four, it is the lowest nature. Animals are instinctive. They have no regret. They are base, cold, calculating, and brutish. Just watch a nature documentary and see how cold and calculating animals are. The stronger animals chase the weaker ones to kill and eat them. They look to destroy the sick and young. They take food from each other, if they can. They show no mercy; they have no court of appeals. It is lion eat gazelle and hyena take from lion ... if he can. No rules; just kill or be killed.

I saved human nature for last because it is unique. Man has a dual nature. He alone possesses it. He shares something in common with animals. He was made from the dust of the ground as they were (Genesis 2:7,19). However, man is not an animal--far from it. You see, man also shares something in common with God. God made man in His image (Genesis 1:26-27). Angels are spiritual beings. Animals are fleshly beings. Humans, alone, are both. We are both physical and spiritual (Matthew 10:28; 1 Thessalonians 5:23). We share the image of God. We have flesh like animals. We alone are made with this unique nature.

God put us over the works of His hands because of our unique creation. We can think, reason, ponder, reflect, and then act.

History shows this to be the case. Men have done great things in this world. This is consistent with our nature. We are spiritual beings. Sadly, because we are fleshly, we can also be base, cold, calculating and even murderous--just like animals. History also shows this to be the case. We have done a lot of evil to one another.

Interestingly, it is just this aspect of human nature that God trusts. Adam was put in the garden to dress it and keep it (Genesis 2:15). God trusted Adam to do the right thing. He honored Adam by giving him options. He gave him the freedom to choose. Adam's choice did not please God, but God trusted Adam and allowed him to make it. God has always trusted His humanity.

Whenever God sought to help humanity, He used humans to help mankind. The reason is simply that man could be trusted. Noah built the ark (Genesis 6:14-17). Abraham received the promises (Genesis 12:1-7). Moses delivered Israel (Exodus 3:1-14). Joshua conquered the land (Joshua 1:1-10). Esther became queen (Esther 4:14-16). Hannah received Samuel (1 Samuel 1). Mary bore Jesus (Matthew 1:18-25). You need to know how much God trusts you. He trusts you to do the right thing.

He gave you His Word because He trusts you to read It. He trusts you to understand It and apply It to your life. We should all be happy that God trusts us. He does not micromanage us. He empowers us and then trusts us to live the life. He has crowned you with glory and honor, and He has set you over the works of His hands because He has complete confidence in you. If He told you to do something, be assured that He has empowered you to do it.

The Fourth is Preeminence

The next phrase of the angel indicates man's place in God's creation. The phrase is "you have put all things under his feet." The phrase indicates the preeminence of humanity in God's creation. In the Psalm the angel states that all of the material creation and all of the animals are below man. Animals are not equal to man--never have been, never will be. Some humans have misplaced their care for animals by their exaltation of animals.

We should be kind and compassionate to animals. A wise man will care for the feelings of his animals; however, it must be understood by all, that human beings are superior to animals. We share the image of God, animals do not. We have immortal souls; animals do not. We are crowned with glory and honor. We are set over the works of God's hands. All things on earth are set under humanity, including animals.

Human beings are the zenith of God's creation. Human beings are intelligent. Human beings train animals, not the other way around.

I actually heard of some people getting into cages and being put on display to relate to animals. This is about the same as a person who can walk sitting in a wheel chair for a while; sitting in a wheel chair is not the same as being confined to a wheelchair if you can get up anytime you want. I am not sure how much more absurd one could get: Humans walking into cages and out of cages anytime they choose will not allow them to relate to animals.

When have a group of animals gone into a city and caged a bunch of humans, then have taken them back to the jungle and put them on display. When has any animal brought a circus with trained human beings to the jungle? When has any animal taught a human being to speak? When has any animal processed food for humans to consume? James says that every animal is trained of men, not the other way around (James 3:7).

We should not be cruel to animals, but if we have to choose between humans eating or animals living, then humans must eat. Humans are more important, more significant, and more valuable than animals. After all, of whom are the animal rights group comprised? Oh, yes, humans. Where are the animal rights groups for animals? There is no animal delegation going to Washington. It is foolish to exalt animals to equality with humans, though some actually believe animals are superior to man.

This likely comes as a result, of humans referring to themselves as animals. You are not an animal! You are made in the image of God. You are crowned with glory and honor. You are made a little lower than angels, which is way higher than apes. Young people make sure you get this: You are not an animal. Listen to God, not to confused humans who have forgotten their Maker. Allow God and His Word to shape your thoughts about yourself. You are made a little lower than angels!

This is the reason taking human life is far more serious than taking the life of animals. No one goes on trial for killing ants. No one is called into question for swatting a fly. No one is called into court for fishing and eating the catch. No one is held over on bail for killing gnats, bees, wasps, roaches, deer, elk, cows, or chickens; however, when Adolph Hitler murdered millions of human beings, those who participated in the atrocities were held responsible.

They were tried; many were convicted and jailed or even executed. Even if one should be found today of having participated in Nazi War Crimes he would yet be tried, why? Because despite the strange conceptions of some, despite the misinformation and propaganda we are fed every day, every one really knows humans are more important, significant, and superior to animals, for human beings share the image of God.

What This Means to You

Here is what all of this means, and this is why you should be happy about what the angel observed. What he saw means that you have been empowered by God to accomplish everything that God expects of you. You are not empowered to be a great musician or athlete; that takes talent. If you cannot sing or jump, do not wait for God to empower you to do those kinds of things--they are physical. Instead go practice or hire someone to teach you. What God expects of you is spiritual and this means that you are in control of your life. Your tongue does not move or speak without your controlling it. You can love your enemies and live like Christ. You are not destined to misery so please do not resign yourself to sadness.

You are not a customer service employee void of power; rather you are the CEO of your life. You can eat what you want to eat, stop what you want to stop and start what you want to start. It is within your power to overcome bad habits and start good habits. Every believer can learn to be like our heavenly Father. You can love your fellow man and light the world around you.

Instead of complaining that there is nothing good on television, turn it off or change the channel. You can control what goes into your mind. Instead of talking about people talking about people, you stop doing it and maybe others will follow. You are empowered by God! You are not a slave to your appetite. You can stop eating things that are not good for you. You can learn what is and what is not good for you.

By the power and grace of God spiritually there is nothing beyond your ability. You can stop lying and start telling the truth.

Stop stealing and go to work and give things to people. You are not a slave to your passions nor are you out of control. You are not powerless you are empowered, in Christ you can. You can have a great marriage. You can be great parents.

Your children can grow up to love God, and their neighbors as themselves. You can forgive and start over. You can say you are sorry. You can be vulnerable. You can give your whole heart away to another. You can even overcome the pain of having it broken. You can come back to God. You can choose. You can start living differently today. You can do all of this and more. You can be happy! Why? Because happiness comes from knowing that God has empowered you to do everything He expects of you.

Happiness is spiritual. Remember when you were young: Did you think a lot about heaven? Did you not want to go and see all of the amazing things? Did you not want to see and be with God forever? It is a sad day for Christianity when we live and long more for this earth than we do heaven.

I want to go to heaven, do you? Read this next chapter with me and let us take a trip there together. When we know we are going to heaven, we can be happy on earth.

What Do You Think?

1. What are the four natures revealed in Scripture?
2. Compare Jesus and angels (Hebrews 1)?
3. How does humanity compare to the rest of creation (Matthew 16:26)?
4. What one is willing to pay for something indicates the worth of that item; concerning redemption, what does that mean man is worth?
5. What four things did the angel observe about us?
6. Are humans animals or a little lower than angels?
7. What demonstrates that man is crowned with glory and honor? How does that make you feel?
8. What does being empowered by God mean?

Chapter 12

A Picture of Heaven

"God Wants You in Heaven, Do You Want to Go?"

Clear your mind for just a second and imagine you are walking on a long winding road. It is a beautiful road. It is smoothly paved; it is bright and clear. You stoop down to get a closer look and the street appears to be made of gold. Ahead in the distance, you see a castle. On either side of the road you see tall, lush, green vegetation. Trees abound, yielding all kinds of fruit. The fruit and the flowers are beautiful.

You stop and stare because the colors are especially vivid. The reds are redder, and the blues are more vibrant and sharper than anything you have ever seen. Yellow has never looked as bright, nor green as crisp as here. Never have flowers smelled so fresh. Never has fruit looked so ripe and sweet. Things are very familiar, yet peculiar and strange.

Each step you take leads you closer to the amazing castle ahead of you. As you near it, you notice movement. At the moment, you are too far away to tell what it is. As you draw nearer, you notice the movement is the result of living beings. They are odd looking but not scary, strange yet majestic. You stop and stare; you wipe your eyes; you strive to focus. You pinch yourself and it hurts; yes, you are awake.

Some of these beings are walking, and some are actually flying. They have wings. Clear, transparent, gorgeous wings. Some have two, some four, some six. They appear to be made of light, and even though you have never seen one, you know right away these are angels. One approaches you and greets you. You ask the most obvious, and what seems the most important question, "Where am I?"

A long pause ensues as he looks at you. "You are in heaven, he responds, and I am your angel."

You faint. After you awake, he says, "I will be your guide. I will show you around. I know you have many questions and I will answer them as we go." You enter the gate. There are actually twelve gates. Each gate is made of one pearl. The street is made of gold. Once you are inside of the gates, you approach the castle. You notice the door is made of pure light. The angel leads you into a great hall. It is full of activity! Angels are busily flying about. Everyone is moving so fast, but they never impede each other. Their movements are in perfect harmony. There are all kinds of them.

You marvel at their precision and their busy pace. You stand in awe--your mouth wide open, and the angel says, "This is the hub of heaven. These angels are on missions from God. There are different angels with different tasks. There are angels of war. They are the army of God. They execute judgment from God. There goes one now. I will show you the armory later. Those are cherubs over there," he points to another group of angels, without so much as a pause he continues, "And over there are seraphs. Some praise and adore God for He is Holy." You can scarcely catch your breath. He continues as if this were normal for you, "There are many rooms here and many other angels. ..."

Unable to hold your tongue any longer you interrupt, "This is amazing; it is beautiful, magnificent, wonderful incredible." You search for word after word to describe it and each one seems as unsatisfactory as the last.

You are further amazed when the angel says, "Hold on this is simply the hall. We have not even started the tour yet. If you are ready then we will begin."

Your senses are on fire. You are alive like you have never been. "Yes, oh yes!" you shout, "but I could stay here and be satisfied."

Then he says, with a smile, "You are in for a treat." He leads you down a hall and the tour begins. "We will enter some rooms, and others we will not. Above each door will be a title of what goes on in the room, for instance, this door is marked cloud making."

The angels ask if you understand.

"Of course, of course," you respond, "I understand."

Then let us continue, "This room is the armory that I said I would show you. As angels, we fight evil. Whenever God calls, we come here to arm ourselves. That angel I pointed out to you earlier is of the heavenly host. They defend and protect. Notice their battle armor. See the swords; look, but do not touch. You will hurt yourself if you are not trained. The swords are light; they are able to pierce and divide to the soul. Once we had an uprising here. Once!" He continues, "This room is the great banquet hall." The hall is huge. The ceiling is made of stars, actual stars and galaxies. The room is full of lush green vegetation. There in the midst of the room is a street. On either side of the street is a river. He resumes, "Yes, there are trees. Each tree yields twelve kinds of fruit."

"What is that the angels are eating?" you ask.

"It is Manna, its angel's food." He continues, "That tree over there is the tree of life. It bears twelve kinds of fruit."

Through the banquet hall you go. "There, what is that door?" you ask. The door is marked "Dungeon."

The angel grabs you, "We will not go through that door that door leads to outer darkness. It is a place reserved for rebellious angels. Remember that uprising I told you about? Those who followed wickedness were put there."

You go through room after room. Every room seems more amazing than the last. There is a room marked "Creation." "What is this room, and what does it mean?" you ask.

Your guide responds, "This is where we see God's creation, would you like to look inside."

"Absolutely!" you shout.

He opens the door and you notice the joy of the angel as he talks, "Look at the sun, moon and stars. The stars are incredible he says." You strain to see as he continues to talk. "The sun is fire and light," he says. "It is brighter than a thousand million lights."

Refusing to pretend, you interrupt your guide and say, "I cannot see the sun or the moon."

He assures you they are there and they are huge. "It is the size of creation," he says, "that makes them hard for you to see. Stars have different shapes and different sizes." He says, "The stars are without number. Each star is pure energy. Stars strain to burn; they yearn to lighten the darkness." He whispers, "They actually die to give light. It is amazing, they give their life to give light." He continues, "Sometimes, we angels come here and just marvel at God's handy-work. We are amazed at the detail and beauty. We spend our free moments here looking at the wonder of His wisdom. We talk among ourselves about His intricate detail. He thought of everything. We think of it as one of God's greatest works."

You continue, and reach a door marked, "Throne Room." You pause. "Is this is the throne room?" you ask.

"Yes, it is," says the angel.

"Are we actually going to go into the throne room of ..."

Before you can finish, he answers, "Yes, we are."

You try to steady yourself before you go in. You go through the door and angels surround the throne. He resumes, "These are the angels of praise and glory. They surround God's throne and shout, 'Holy, Holy, Holy, Lord God Almighty.' God is worthy of praise," he says.

"Of course, of course," you say softly.

Within the throne room, there is a street. "This street is called 'The Way,'" he answers.

You notice that a river runs on either side of the street. You ask what it is.

"It is the river of the water of life," he says, "It is clear as crystal."

You try to focus, but you cannot because your mind is so full of questions that you can no longer restrain yourself. You feel like a cracked dam that has been straining to hold back a flood. Your words fly out of your mouth faster than bullets out of a Gatling gun. They stumble over each other and you begin to shoot out, "Will we see God? How many angels are there? How many rooms are there? Do you ever get tired? Have you ever asked yourself why God made you? Have you ever wanted to be something other than what you are? Is there any sorrow here; are you ever sad? What is the purpose of it all?"

The angel struggles to stop you. "Slow down, slow down, and I will answer your questions," he says softly trying to calm you down. "Will we see God? Yes. How many angels are there? There is an innumerable host of angels. There are many kinds of angels we could not see them all. Each of us has different functions. No, we never get tired. Sorrow, and sadness, I do not think you would understand. We love God we serve freely. Have I ever wanted to be something other than I am, no why would I? Now about your last question," he pauses, "What is the purpose of it all? Of all of your questions it may be the most difficult to answer." He continues, "We know much, but we do not know everything. You have seen the immense size and scope of the castle. You have seen the beauty and splendor of many things here. You have seen the glorious rooms with each door yielding more adventure and wonder than the last. You have seen the angels the multitude of angels. They all have different shapes, sizes and missions. You have seen the creation that glorious magnificent creation. It is God's signature. We wonder and marvel at its glory and splendor. And you ask, 'Why? Why, what is the purpose of it all?' I will tell you this: We have wondered that as well. We have wondered what we are doing on these missions and what God is doing. We have inquired and we are certainly interested. We all are sure God will tell us one day, but as it is no one knows."

You are devastated. Your head falls. Your eyes well up with tears.

And the angel says, "I can tell you are anxious, I wish I knew more but I do not; however, I will tell you what I know." You perk up; you wipe your eyes; you listen intently as he says, "God has a special project. He gives it a lot of His attention and care. He protects it and watches over it very carefully. We do not know everything about it, because God has not told us. You know, no being can know the mind of God; not even us unless He reveals it to us. We know God made it, because He showed us. We know when He made it, because He told us. Sometimes He sends us on errands to it. Even He has gone to visit it. But what He is doing? I, we, well, no one knows. We know He protects it and watches over it. No one here questions God. However, compared to all you have seen, we do not know what He sees in it. I do believe it has to do with our purpose, and the purpose behind all you have seen, and all that exists."

"What? What is it?" you shout.

He continues, "I could show you better than I could tell you. Remember the creation room?" he asks.

"Yes, yes, I remember," you reply.

"We did not see it all." He leads you back to the creation room. As he opens the door he says, "Here is where light lives. The way to light's house is this way. Yes, light lives just over there. Here is where God keeps darkness. The sun sleeps over there. Here is where God formed the stars. They are without number." With hand outstretched, he says, "Behold, God's creation."

You are in awe, you cannot believe your eyes; no wonder you were smiling when we first came in. No wonder you think it is God's signature. "It is amazing," you respond.

As you try to take it all in, he interrupts you and says, "That is not it." He beckons you closer and says, "Now, look past the galaxies; look past the constellations. Look past all of those things. Do you see it?"

You stretch and strain, but you cannot see what he is talking about. "No, no, I do not see it," you insist. Please, please show me. I want to know, I need to know!" you shout out. "Tell me what you are talking about. I thought this was it!" you insist.

Frustrated, your guide says, "I knew this would be difficult, I just knew it," he says. "There right there down there, there do you see that little speck? Look closer, look harder; it is right there; it is a little tiny speck, but it is there" he assures you. Finally he says, "Give me your hand."

He takes your hand and points, He places it on something you can barely see. "This little, almost invisible, tiny dot?" you ask.

"Yes," he says, relieved you have finally found it. He looks at you and says, "Now you have found the sun. From here," he motions, "count three dots and you are there."

He enlarges your view and you recognize it instantly. You gasp! Now screaming, bordering on hysteria, you continue, "All of this ... all of this is ... for that? I do not believe it. This place, heaven itself; all of those angels and all of that activity was for ... God's project is earth?" Your voice climbs ever higher. You shake your head as you say it again, "The angels and all of those rooms are working for God's project?" Still pointing, you ask again, "That is God's project?" Refusing to accept it, you continue--as if saying it again will change it, "This room, the creation room, all that is in this room: the sun, moon, and stars, the galaxies, everything. I cannot believe it. God watches over this? This is what God is intimately concerned about? He cares, He watches over, He protects, He loves earth?"

Before you can still your mind, the angel chimes in, "I see you are as surprised as we were. We could not believe it either. And I will tell you something else," he says, "We have actually seen God sad about it; can you imagine that? Can you imagine an infinitely loving Being, sad? And can you imagine how we feel when God is sad? Can you imagine how we feel when God hurts? I have seen God sad myself. And, oh, how it made me sad. And it is all over, well, that. We trust God and love Him. We know what He does is best, but only God knows what He is doing. He has not told us. Still, I will tell you that we have wondered. We have inquired, but it is not what you think. All of this is not for earth. No, there are plenty of planets. It is for those who live there. God calls him man."

The angel's words hit you like a ton of bricks. You are standing, but you have no feelings in your legs. You are sure that you have fainted. Like a television gone off for the night, your mind becomes snow. You cannot see or hear a thing. All you can do is think and your thinking has never been clearer.

Immediately, you think of your life; in an instant you hear every word you have ever said. How often had you complained and how long had you lived with doubt. You think about all the days you felt unsafe and unsure about your relationship with God. You think of how lonely and how distant you have always felt from God.

You think about your prayers. How often you felt He was not there, how often you felt He did hear, and how often you wondered if He really cared. You think of everything that you believed to be important. You think of all the people you know and how many of them feel and behave the same way you did.

You know the angel is still talking, but you cannot hear a thing; all you can do is think. You are confused and delighted. You are rejoicing and ashamed. You know he is talking, but you can barely hear him. Hearing him is like trying to see on a dark night through a dense fog.

You can barely hear his voice as he continues, "We do not know a lot about man. We do know that God made him. We rejoiced at God's creation. We know that we work on man's behalf." It is as if the angel notices that you are barely there; he draws closer. Looking more serious, he makes sure you are focused before he resumes. "One time," he says looking intently at you, "an angel was looking down at man [he was probably in this very room], and he turned to God and said:

> When I look at your heavens, the work of your fingers, the moon and the stars, which you have set in place, what is man that you are mindful of him, and the son of man, that care for him? Yet you have made him a little lower than the heavenly beings, and crowned him with glory and honor. You have given him dominion over the works of your hands; you have put all things under his feet, all sheep and oxen, and also the beasts of the field, the birds of the heavens, and the fish of the sea, whatever passes along the paths of the seas. O LORD, our Lord, how majestic is your name in all the earth!

The angel continues, "This is as close as we can get to understanding the purpose of it all. Everything that you have seen and all of us angels, in some measure, exists because God created man. Like God, all of us angels have only wished that man knew how much God loves him."

Friend, the next time you go outside, will you look at the creation? And when you do, I want you to think. Think about the grass--each blade is unique; think about the sun--its strength and strategic placement being just far enough away to keep us warm and grow our crops, but not so far away that we freeze to death; think about the seas and oceans and all the living creatures that inhabit them. Think about the birds, and insects, the creeping things, and about all they are and do. Think about the jungles, the Amazon, the rain-forests, and the desserts. Think about all of the animals, big and small. Look up and notice the stars. They cannot be numbered. Consider the sheer magnitude of the sky. Think about the galaxies of which the Milky Way is only one, and when you do, marvel at our ignorance of how vast it all really is.

Think about the angels. Think about their countless missions, their continual service, their grandeur, their beauty, and all of their mighty power. Then, just when you are ready to stop thinking, think about you! Then try, I mean try as hard as you can, to engulf your mind in the thought that all of that, and all that there is, is because God made you.

If you are able to do that, and I pray that you are, then add this thought to it: When we turned our backs on Him, when we snubbed our noses at Him for sin and self, then He laid His only Son upon a cross and killed Him, so that He could have us back!

God loves you; He hopes that you know how much.

"Let not your hearts be troubled. Ye believe in God; believe also in me. In my Father's house are many rooms. If it were no so, would I have told you that I go to prepare a place for you? And if I go and prepare a place for you, I will come again and will take you to myself, that where I am you may be also" (John 14:1-3).

Happiness is knowing that heaven awaits us. This world is not all there is. God did all He did so that we could live with Him in heaven.

What Do You Think?

1. Share your thoughts about heaven.
2. Do you feel like man is God's special project?
3. Discuss Isaiah 45:12-18 ("He formed it to be inhabited")?
4. How does going to heaven impact life on earth?

Chapter 13

A Picture of Happiness

"You can be Happy!"

We are spiritual beings made by God the Father of spirits (Zechariah 12:1). We live in a world within a world. That which we see is the temporal façade; that which we do not see is the eternal reality. We are created beings. We live in a world that was made for us, by God who loves us. God loves us so much that when we rejected Him, He laid His only begotten Son on a cross and sacrificed Him for us. God saves us by His grace. We must have faith in Him. He made us in His image. He wants us in heaven.

There is nothing that will ever change God's love for us, because God never changes. To understand God is the most important thing any of us can do. We should all seek the Lord and find Him. Thankfully, He is not very far from any of us (Acts 17:27). The only way to understand God is to read, study, and meditate upon His Word. Chances are good you have four or five Bibles at home, so you have a great opportunity to do these things.

Armed with the knowledge of God, we will know how to be happy. Happiness is not an imaginary place, neither is happiness a destination to a place. Happiness is real. It is not a state of mind; it is a state of being. The individual is happy. Blessed is the man; or the man is blessed.

Nothing on earth can make you happy. Nothing physical can make you happy. Whatever you buy will get old, wear out, and stop working. There is a reason we have trash heaps. Wherever you go will have the same things you left behind; namely, people, places, and things. Eventually, you will get tired of them in the new place, and that which once made you happy will no longer make you happy.

You cannot fix something physically to make yourself happy. You do not have to fix anything, because nothing is broken. You do not need a house, body, hair, or clothes makeover. There is nothing wrong with you physically. You need a soul makeover. You have been listening to the wrong messages. You are looking for happiness in all the wrong places. Stop listening to the false promises of those who profit from your search. Stop seeking happiness in empty places. Nothing you fix will make you happy. There is nothing physical you can do to fix spiritual problems.

God teaches us how to have a relationship with Him. He calls us His children. He calls Himself our Father. He promised to never leave us. He promised never to forsake us, and He never will. Because He made us in His image, we are crowned with glory and honor. You must stop letting others tell you what you are; rather, listen to God--He made you. No human being is an animal. No human being has ever been an animal. Humans are a little lower than angels; this is never said of any ape.

Sharing God's image makes us worth the whole world. The sun, moon, and stars pale in comparison to you. You are fearfully and wonderfully made. You are made a little lower than the angels. You are set over the works of God's hand. You were worth dying for, so God sent Christ to die.

Happiness is not outside of you, and happiness is not within you waiting to be discovered. Happiness is in God, and God has placed the capacity to find it within you. Happiness is having your sins forgiven. Happiness is knowing that you and God are at peace. Happiness is being in Christ. Your sins are forgiven by the blood of Jesus in your obedience to the Gospel. Those who are buried into His death are forgiven (Romans 6:3-4). This is happiness.

If your sins are forgiven, then you are happy. Nothing physical can remove your sins. God in Christ forgives sins. Of the things written in this book that you must understand, please understand this: If you buy a new car and you are in sin, what do you have? If the car cost twenty-thousand or two hundred thousand, what can it do? You can gas it up and drive it. You can be looked at by people as you drive by. You can park it on the curb or in the garage. You can give it to the valet when you pull up to your favorite spot. When it gets dirty, you can wash it. What can you do other than drive it? Will it make you happy? It will give you temporary joy. You will feel good about having it, but what good is the car if you have no peace? What good is the car if sin rules your life? Cars do not make people become better people. Cars do not forgive sins against God. The car will get old, or maybe it will get wrecked, or maybe it will get stolen. This is why Jesus told us to be careful about what we hold dear:

> Do not lay up for yourselves treasures on earth, where moth and rust destroy and, where thieves break in and steal, but lay up for yourselves treasures in heaven, where neither moth nor rust destroys, and where thieves do not break in and steal: For where your treasure is, there your heart will be also. (Matthew 6:19-21)

Who told you that if you were rich you would be happy, and why do you believe them? Everything on earth is subject to decay. Everything on earth can be destroyed or stolen. The Lord is telling us not to put our happiness in anything here. If heaven is the source of our happiness, then you should stop being sad and turning against God when something happens to your things on earth. God is good even if your child is sick, your boss is lousy, your spouse is cheating, or you best friend lied on you. God's goodness is not diminished by human behavior. God is good, period. God is good if a storm destroys your house, a drunk driver hits you, or your child gets on drugs. God's goodness is not determined by the quietness of your life. God was good before He made man on the sixth day, because God is good eternally.

You are a spiritual being. Your greatest need is spiritual. If you lay up your treasure here, whatever you choose will fail; however, if your treasure is in heaven, then nothing can touch it or take it away. Forgiveness of sins cannot be affected by things on earth. Salvation does not rust or corrupt. Forgiveness cannot be stolen; it cannot decay. If your iniquity is forgiven, if your transgression is covered, then you are happy.

It does not matter where the happy man goes, because neither the journey nor the destination made him happy. If one is happy, it will not matter where he goes, because he is happy before he gets there; conversely, if a man is unhappy, he will be unhappy no matter where he goes, because he is unhappy before he gets there. If a man does not have his sins forgiven, he can never truly be happy. He can have temporary moments of joy, but not lasting happiness. He will never be better than Solomon who found that all was vanity.

If your relationship with God is solid, then you are happy, or blessed. Will the storms of life come to your house? Yes! Will your house stand when they come? Yes! It does not matter what you lose, or what is taken from you. It does not matter who is taken from you. Nothing on earth can take your joy, because nothing on earth gave it.

Here is how to be happy: You can be happy if you know that God made the world with you in mind, and if you live in the world with God in mind! If after reading all of this you still look at your situation and conclude but I am still in an unhappy situation. My husband is still a bad husband, or my wife is still a bad wife. Or maybe my child is still on drugs or pregnant or I still need more money. If whatever your situation is leads you to conclude I am still unhappy. Then take it easy on yourself, Rome was not built in a day. Repetition is the key to learning, so read the book again, and again. You can be happy in the place you are in, that situation is not the thermostat for your happiness God is.

What Do You Think?

1. Explain how happiness is not under the sun; it is beyond the sun.
2. What will man find wherever he goes?
3. Does man need a makeover to make him happy? If so, what kind?
4. Discuss this idea: You take you wherever you go; therefore, if you are not happy, it will not matter where you go.

ABOUT THE AUTHOR

Eric Owens is the pulpit minister for the Avondale church of Christ in Decatur, Georgia. He has preached there since 1997. Eric also serves as an elder for Avondale congregation since 2009. He and his wife, Vanessa, have three daughters, Brittany (Davis), Breania, and Bethany. Eric is an ex-marine having served our nation and participated in the first Gulf War. He holds many gospel meetings and speaks at many lectureships around the country. Brother Owens graduated from a two-year intensive preacher training program at the Memphis School of Preaching in 1994. He is also a graduate of Amridge University (2001) with a Bachelor of Science Degree. Eric and his family live in Snellville, Georgia.